Published by: Lakhani Publishing

Copyright © 2011 by Lakhani Publishing
All Rights Reserved

Lakhani Jayendra
Forex Mastery a Child's Play
ISBN: 978-0-9568236-0-1

Printed in the United Kingdom for worldwide distribution

The material in this book is designed to provide accurate and authoritative information in regard to Forex trading strategies which the author has used for many years.

This book is being sold on the basis that the publisher is not engaged in giving legal, accounting or other professional service. The reader should consult their professional advisers. The contents of this book are purely for educational purpose.

DEDICATION

This book is dedicated to the *immense power that lies within YOU*, to achieve forex mastery. Success is yours, if that is your Core Desire.

I also dedicate this book to my parents to whom I shall remain indebted for setting the foundation, and also to my children, Bhavesh, Beena, Anand and the little princess Bindal, for their love and support.

Wishing you all abundance of love & happiness – for when you have this two, Wealth will always be attracted to you.

God Bless

Jayendra Lakhani

Contents

PART 1 – TRADING PSYCHOLOGY

PART 2 – TRADING SYSTEM & PLAN

PART 3 – THE POWER WITHIN

ABOUT THE AUTHOR

Jayendra Lakhani was born in Malawi, Central Africa and came to the UK when he was 18. He is a professional trader and has been involved with markets since his early twenties. He has extensive experience in trading international markets - derivatives, Forex, Index & Stock futures, and Commodities.

Jayendra's trading career started in the Mid 80's and he has survived a number of stock market crashes, including the crash of 1987 – an experience that has made him a better trader today. Over the years, he has developed unique trading systems and strategies, which have made him into a successful trader, trading mentor and author.

One would say that Jayendra is blessed with a mind that finds creative solutions to problems; a kind of a person that sees multiple solutions, he has a very inquisitive mind. Once he devises a trading strategy, he will always look at ways at which it can be improved. Jayendra uses Technical Analysis in his trading, and believes that successful trading is based on your Strategies and Mental Fitness – your system. He believes that more emphasis should be put on trader psychology and having a disciplined money management approach.

Jayendra is also the Internet's foremost Forex coach and mentor, and teaches his system to individual investors. For more information about his training and mentoring programme, full details are on our website: www.4x4u.net.

Jayendra has been involved in **Live Trading workshops** and Seminars worldwide - USA, Canada, United Kingdom, Switzerland, United Arab Emirates, India and many other countries.

Prior to becoming a full time trader, Jayendra was an Accountant, having worked with large companies such as British Airways and Visionhire – a Granada Company. Later on, Jayendra also worked as a Financial Planner specialising in Portfolio Management and Tax Planning.

ONE TO ONE WITH JAYENDRA LAKHANI

A three month personalised mentoring programme that is designed and specifically tailored for YOU as an individual and to suit your style of trading. It is my mission to create a community of successful forex traders, and I will help you to get trading profitably and consistently.

More details - **http://www.4x4u.net/one2one2.asp**

VIDEO BASED MENTORING SERVICE

Over 150+ library of video tutorials, in addition a new video is uploaded each at regular intervals.

More details - **http://www.4xmentor.net/**

COME INTO MY TRADING ROOM

We also offer LIVE forex Signal Chats, giving you buy/Sell signals in real time

http://www.4x4u.net/fxalerts.asp

ACKOWLEDGEMENTS

Many, many people have gone into the making of this book. First and foremost, I would like to thank my family, especially my adorable children Bhavesh, Beena, Anand and the little princess Bindal. Whilst it might be trite to thank the family members who did none of the research nor write any of the words, without their support, this book would not have been possible.

I would like to thank esignal.com, for the permission to reprint charts from their charting package. Thank you to Joy Khambhaita for helping me with the layout and formatting of the book, to Anup Deshpande for designing the cover.

Special thanks to Vinod Gohil, who as a friend was probably the first person i fully trained and introduced him to trading, it was his inspiration that made me realise the teaching capabilities I had.

Special thanks also goes to all the attendees to my first ever live trading seminar in Canada and USA in 2007, as it was due to their request for me to do a seminar for them, that resulted into me writing this book. Some of the attendees have gone on to become professional traders, money managers and my competitors – Forex trainers and mentors. It truly goes on to show that Trading Mastery is a Child's Play, if you know what you doing.

I would also like to thank a number of my colleagues and friends, who have come up with ideas and suggestions not only in writing this book, but also for the inspiration and confidence that I have received from them when trading, often exchanging ideas and strategies and giving each other the moral support. Trading can be very lonely at times.

In my opinion, success in trading is 90% Psychology. In my own trading career, I owe a great deal to so many teachers who have come and changed my life for better, thus giving me strong mental fitness enabling me to balance the emotions of fear and greed, and able to follow my trading plan with discipline.

Finally, my thanks to you, the readers of this book. No doubt you have taken a big step from the crowd of amateurs, by purchasing this book you have resolved to become a successful trader. I am sure you will not be disappointed and soon you will be on a path to being a successful trader. God bless.

Jayendra Lakhani

"Don't wait for extraordinary opportunities. Seize common occasions and make them great. Weak men wait for opportunities; strong men make them."

Orison Swett Marden

PREFACE

"There are powers within you which, if you would use them consistently will eventually lead you to mastery."
Jayendra Lakhani

Many people just go through their day to day life and simply accept whatever fate brings them. A few would succeed by accident but most suffer frustration and unhappiness. They simply do not have the willpower or the commitment to make the change.

This book is dedicated to your success in mastery of life and Forex trading. The simple fact that you are reading this book indicates that you have the will and desire to live a life better than you have now.

Having top strategies and rules, excitement from trading the markets will not guarantee success, so FOLLOW and ACT on your golden rules to make your trading more bankable.

For example one of your golden rules could be:

- Trade with the trend - No Trend, No Trade!
- Plan the trade – Trade the plan!
- Buy at support, sell at resistance!

The list is endless, but you should ideally get a short list of at least 10 rules. Display your golden rules in your office or trading area, and read it every day.

The Bollywood film "GURU" is said to be a biopic on the life of late Indian Industrialist Dhirubhai Ambani. The film is very inspirational, emotional and uplifting. I have been inspired by the life of a great man. Dhirubhai Ambani inspires everyone from all walks of life, that every person can make their dreams come true. You dream big and make your dream come true finally, because you know what your dreams and ambitions are.

"For those who dare to dream, there is a whole world to win!"
- Dhirubhai Ambani

Trading is an art, an art of reading the charts and spotting the signals, managing risk and letting the profits run. Having to minimize your loss and maximize your profit requires mental fitness.

This book gives you the tools of methodology, planning the trade and the mental aspect of trading – how to build strong mental fitness. Using plain English, dynamic pictures and real life trade examples, this book makes it easy for you to achieve Trading Mastery. You will be amazed how quickly you will learn.

By the time you finish the book, you will realize that forex mastery is truly a child's play.

MASTER TRADER IDENTITY

Some of the "KEY" characteristics of a Master Trader;

- Trades the plan

- Has sound money management rules

- Monitors and manages open positions

- Cuts losses & lets profits run

- Looks for low risk, high probability trade

- Learns from their trading journal

RISK WARNING & DISCLAIMER

Risk Warning

It should be understood that Currency trading involves high risk and you can lose a lot of money. There is always a relationship between high reward and high risk. Any type of market or trade speculation that can yield an unusually high return on investment is subject to unusually high risk. Only surplus funds should be placed at risk and anyone who does not have such funds should not participate in trading foreign currencies. Currency trading is not suitable for everyone.

The strategies discussed in this book are for educational purpose, and are not intended to replace individual research or licensed investment advice. Unique experiences and past performances do not guarantee future results. Testimonials are not representative of all clients. Certain accounts may have worse performance than those indicated or alluded to. Trading currencies involves substantial risk, and there is always the potential for loss. Your trading results may vary.

No representation is being made that these products, and any associated advice or training, will guarantee profits, or not result in losses from trading. Neither the products, any explanation or demonstration of their operation, nor any training held in conjunction therewith, including, without limitation, through online chat, in conjunction with our advertising and promotional campaigns, during our in-person seminars or otherwise, should be construed as providing a trade recommendation or the giving of investment advice. The purchase, sale or advice regarding a currency can only be performed by a licensed Broker/Dealer. Neither I, nor any of my affiliates or associates, is a registered Broker/Dealer or Investment Advisor in any State or Federally-sanctioned jurisdiction. You are encouraged to consult with a licensed professional adviser regarding any particular trade or trading strategy.

THIS INFORMATION IS PROVIDED FOR EDUCATIONAL/ INFORMATIONAL PURPOSES ONLY. PAST OR HYPOTHETICAL PERFORMANCE IS NOT INDICATIVE OF FUTURE RESULTS

WELCOME MESSAGE FROM JAYENDRA LAKHANI

Dear Trader,

Greetings & welcome to this unique course - Forex Mastery – A Child's Play. Lakhani Publishing is privileged to have you as a participant.

The majority of traders fail to succeed, YOU are one of the rare few wanting to join the 5% club of consistent winners, and you have demonstrated this by purchasing this book. We are fully committed to support you in your quest to become a Master Trader – By having a winning trading plan, your odds of success in the markets are increased. Our goal is to create a community of successful Forex Traders.

Let's make a commitment to stay focused and USE the simple trading methodology that you will learn which will change your life forever. I look forward to making a difference to your life – in your journey to become a master trader.

Trade with passion

God Bless and kind regards

Jayendra Lakhani
President - Bindal FX

<u>MY IDENTITY</u>

I always knew
That I was going
To be a successful trader
I NEVER had any doubts.
When I wrote my Trading
Plan, I followed it.
I NEVER doubted my
Plans.
I had BELIEF in my
actions

<u>**Jayendra Lakhani**</u>

PART 1
TRADER
PSYCHOLOGY

Ten Commandments of Trading Success

In order to achieve consistent success in trading Forex and join the 5% club I agree to the following:

1. I will develop a Trading Plan and follow it with ruthless discipline and I will never deviate from it.

2. I will be patient and wait for a low risk / high probability signal to emerge and then pounce. My golden rule is No Signal – No Trade

3. The market rules and I will respect the market and will follow it and not fight it!

4. I will cut my losses when the signal reverses, I will NOT hope and pray when the market goes against me.

5. I will let the winners run, and NOT snatch profits.

6. I will always be motivated and in a positive mindset and focus ONLY on winning. I will think and visualize winning trades and that I am following my trading plan.

7. I will always look for low risk high probability trades and before I pull the trigger I will ensure that I will have at least 3 reasons why I want to trade. I will always look for confluence of indicators.

8. I will focus on my winning trades and will want to duplicate the setup used for future trades; this will then become a habit.

9. I will strengthen my identity daily and invest a minimum of 15 minutes to review my trading journal and diary to learn from it, and also preview the chart potentials for the next day's trades.

10.   I will always stretch myself to achieve extraordinary success and will always seek opportunities by hard work, and work outside my comfort zone.

I have read the above statements and agree to the above. I recognize that I am responsible for my success by the actions that I take. I endeavour to follow my ten commandments of trading success.

I am totally committed to my success as a Forex Trader, and I promise to myself that within 12 months I will have joined the 5% club of consistent winning traders.

I am a winner, I am a successful trader. I set targets and consistently achieve my targets. I am a disciplined trader and I consistently follow my trading guidelines.

Signature:_____   Date:_____

CHAPTER 1

YOUR GOLDEN RULES

"The Golden Rule is of no use to you, unless you take action in accordance with the rule."

Jayendra Lakhani

Golden Rules of Trading

Having top strategies and a trading system alone will not guarantee success, so FOLLOW and ACT on your golden rules to make your trading more bankable. Focus on your Golden Rules enables you to develop a Mental Fitness.

For example one of your "Golden Rules" could be, Trade with the trend: No Trend, No Trade! Or Plan the trade – Trade the plan! Buy at support, sell at resistance!

The list is endless, but you should ideally get a short list of at least 10 rules. Display your golden rules in your office or trading area, and read it every day. You must act upon and follow the golden rules.

What are your TOP 3 Golden Rules?

1.)

2.)

3.)

Do you use your golden rules consistently?

If you do not use your Golden Rules, then why not? Do a self study of what is preventing you to use these Golden Rules?

List 3 reasons why you do not consistently follow your Golden Rules?

1.

2.

3.

BY NOT FOLLOWING YOUR GOLDEN RULES, WHAT IS IT COSTING YOU?

1.

2.

3.

Golden Trading Rules Examples

1. No Signal – No Trade.

2. Plan your trades. Trade your plan.

3. Keep records of your trading results – Keep a trading journal and your Income & Expenditure from trading.

4. Maximise profits, not the number of trades.

5. Be patient enough to wait for good trades.

6. Be patient enough to avoid closing profitable trades too early.

7. Cut losses early, protect profits with trailing stops.

8. Focus on BIG movements. Don't try to catch noisy small fluctuations.

9. Pay attention to price patterns and formations.

10. Don't take the market home.

11. Professional traders buy into bad news and sell into good news.

12. Professional traders have a well-scheduled planned time for studying the markets.

13. Professional traders isolate themselves from the opinions of others.

14. Make your own trading plan.

15. Maintain discipline to be able to constantly suppress bad habits.

16. Success comes with dreams - Dream big dreams and think tall. Very few people set goals too high. A man becomes what he thinks about all day long.

17. Strictly follow my plan and manage my risks.

18. Only I am responsible for my trading result. So If I am wrong, I am to blame, not the market, not the brokers or friends.

19. I will not use excessively tight stop losses – I will spend more time identifying a good entry point, than I will be patient and give the market some freedom and place my stop losses carefully.

20. Always discipline yourself by following a pre-determined set of rules.

21. Know yourself - The key to successful trading is knowing yourself and your stress point.

22. Belief - You must believe in yourself and your judgment if you expect to make a living in this profession.

23. I will commit my mind to the POWERFUL market trend.

24. I will accept losses and move on. Losses are part of the process.

25. Trade with the Trend – I will not try to outguess the markets – I will wait for the reversal to come.

26. I will break my trades in 2 or 4 parts and then withdraw profits gradually, whilst moving the stops on the profit.

27. I will not follow the crowd, because they are usually wrong.

28. Big movements take time to develop, so I will have patience and wait for a perfect setup.

29. I will avoid negative friends – I have learnt the hard way. They will pull you down at every available opportunity.

30. Money can be made every day in the market. There are tons of opportunities, you have to spot them.

31. Forget the news, remember the chart – I do not have the resources and the expertise to know what particular news will have an impact on the price, but the chart already knows that the news is coming. (This is the authors view, having said that, there are many successful traders who focus on fundamentals only with little or no emphasis on technical analysis.)

32. When there is a strong trend in place, I will buy the first pullback from a new high, and sell the first pullback from a new low.

33. Price has a memory – what did the price do the last time it hit a certain level? Chances are it will do it again.

34. Beat the crowd – I will take their money before they take mine. When I trade I am really trading against a crowd, not the currency – that is just a medium. (This is rule is based on the fact that 90% of traders lose money)

35. Trade with a plan-not with hope, greed, or fear. Plan where you will get in the market, how much you will risk on the trade, and where you will take your profits.

36. Watch for divergences in price action with the indicators, such as MACD, RSI and Stochastic.

37. You are your biggest mentor - Analyse your losses. Learn from your losses. They're expensive lessons; you paid for them. Most traders don't learn from their mistakes because they don't like to think about them.

38. Always use stop orders, always...always...always.

39. Never add to a losing position.

40. Fundamental News – Be interested in the market's reaction to news rather than the news itself.

SUMMARY & ACTION POINTS

1.) Most work on spirituality does emphasis on Golden Rules for example the Biblical Verse "Do unto others as you would have them do unto you" (Matthew 7:12)

2.) The 10 Commandments are Rules, which enables one to focus on the self, change starts within the self. We spend so much time cleaning our homes, and clothing, and outer bodies, but our hearts are festering with evil thoughts of people - envy and jealousy, anger and hatred - very destructive emotions. The heart is the seat of knowledge and feelings, and a diseased one causes the entire body to suffer.

3.) Having a set of Golden Rules can guide your behavior in a positive way as it will constantly remind you of your trading rules.

4.) Write your top Golden Rules for Life and for your Business?

CHAPTER 2
THE KISS PRINCIPLE

"I just keep it simple. I aim for maximum effect with minimum means. Watch the charts, analyse the price action and trade it on merit."

Jayendra Lakhani

What does KISS stand for?
The KISS is an abbreviation of Keep It Stupidly Simple or Keep It Simple, Stupid.

What does that mean to a Trader?
I owe my success as a trader to the KISS principle; many traders tend to overcomplicate matters on their analysis for a potential trade, often using many complex indicators leading to analysis paralysis.

Typically when a Forex trader is faced with a potential trade, he often will look at so many indicators, listen to so many gurus, seek opinions of other traders – eventually the trader may either procrastinate and will not trade due to confusion, or may end up trading when the entry is not right!

You can easily devise a simple trading system with just MACD, trend lines and EMAs. Trading can be so easy and can literally be a child's play. But because it sounds so easy – many traders will not follow the basic principles.

How can you apply the KISS principle to trading?

Keeping it simple, is a matter of patience and discipline, mostly with yourself – and that is why it is always better to understand yourself first, before attempting to understand the markets.

Be humble; don't think of yourself as a master trader, this is the first mistake many traders make. Accept that simple strategies will work wonders. You do not need rocket science to succeed.

Focus on no more than three or four indicators on your charts – this can be MACD, Moving averages, support and resistance tools (pivots, Fibonacci and trend lines) – just focusing on these can enable you to consistently bank 1000 pips per month.

Once you become as expert in reading the price action, you will find that you can just trade the markets with absolutely no indicators, maybe just some moving averages and the just price action only.

Technical Analysis Secrets

As I have often said the chart knows everything, it is a clever way to make substantial profits from the markets. The chart is simply a reflection of the Investor mood and emotions, through which it measures the greed and fear emotions. Equilibrium of price is reached through the demand & supply of a commodity.
There is simply no need for a complex and expensive charting package, and often paying through the nose for having so many features would be a waste of money. The "secrets" that are very important from any chart are;

Trend

What is the direction of the price, you must always trade the trend, and never fight the markets, as always go with the flow. The market will go where it wants to go. The simplest identifier of a trend is higher highs in an up trend and lower lows in a downtrend. Often a 13 EMA can be a good measure for a trend. Your simple system should be able to guide you on how to trade the trend and let the profits run for as long as possible.

Support & Resistance

A trading system without support & resistance would be doomed for a failure, as these represent the key junctures where the forces of demand & supply meet. Support is a level where the price stalls and reverses, and this is a buying opportunity. Resistance is a level at which selling is strong, which prevents the price from rising further.

Complex Indicators

Many traders spend countless hours trying to master such complex indicators as Gann, Elliott, Fibonacci or Bollinger bands, without understanding the basic importance of trend or support & resistance. In my opinion there is no need to learn these complex methods that often leading to confusion. The KISS principle should be your guiding principle. Making money from the markets is a child's play and can be achieved with simple tools. My approach is using these simple charts indicators – trend, support & resistance and moving averages.

Knowledge & Skill

A little knowledge can be dangerous, most traders start using complex indicators after attending a weekend seminar! I have seen many traders have their trading accounts wiped out for following a trading system that they did not fully understand, would you ever run a business on very limited knowledge?

Trading Plan

If you fail to plan, you are planning to fail. Majority of traders do not have a trading plan. My training & mentoring service is focused totally around developing a winning trading plan. From my feedback, those traders with a plan tend to be successful traders. Your trading plan must incorporate such areas as

a.) Study of self – YOU, your mindset.
b.) Risk Management;
c.) Methodology – your trading system.

Managing Risk

Managing your risk is the most important element of a successful trader, because it will limit your losses and preserve the capital. The key is to keep losses small and let the profits run. It is also very important to trade in the proportion of your trading account and have realistic expectations. Do not overtrade your account!

Making money from the markets is easy and can be a child's play, and I can assure you that trading can lead to easy money – yet it is amazing how many traders mess it up, it is well accepted that 90% of traders fail. If you learn fully the trading basics and follow the KISS principle, it will enable you to trade well and profitably – it will change your life forever, for you can truly become a master trader, without having a PhD. Thus joining the 5% winner club.

Advantages of keeping it Simple

1. Because of its simplicity, you are able to understand it better and quickly identify trade setups.

2. As a result you begin to trust the setups – You gain belief.

3. This leads to confidence in following the trading plan – End result = PROFIT!

SUMMARY & ACTION POINTS

1.) KISS is an acronym, and the some of the different variations are: – Keep it simple stupid, keep it short and simple, keep it simple and straightforward.

2.) Think of ways how you can apply KISS principle to trading.

3.) Concentrate on simple strategies what work, without over complicating the matter. What simple strategies can you use?

4.) The more complicated a trading system, the higher the chances that it may fail.

5.) Complicated trading strategies can be counterproductive, as often over analysis can lead to the paralysis of your thought process.

"Our life is frittered away by detail. Simplicity, simplicity, simplicity! I say, let your affairs be as two or three, and not a hundred or a thousand; instead of a million count half a dozen, and keep your accounts on your thumb-nail. Simplify, simplify."

Henry David Thoreau

"Simple strategies work best, because they allow you to trade with confidence, and if you trade with confidence, you are a step closer to eliminating the emotion of fear from your trading"

Jayendra Lakhani

CHAPTER 3
PARALYSIS
ANALYSIS

"The maxim 'Nothing but perfection' may be spelled paralysis."

Winston Churchill

Are You Suffering From.... Paralysis of Analysis?

Do you have a good trading methodology and great ideas, but just when it came down to the final step....you felt that you needed to "add this" or "change that", or "just tweak it a little more".
You "tweaked" it until you tweaked it out! It was never quite right. The results..... You never implemented your trading methodology. A case of .....Paralysis of Analysis.

Analysis paralysis is where you are unable to make any progress moving forward because you bog yourself down in details, tweaking, brainstorming and spending so much time in perfecting the system that you are unable to take any action.
Your trading system will not be perfect, in fact it will never be perfect – you just have to be ready and have confidence in your system and then FIRE. The point is to TAKE ACTION and to move you forward. You can always go back and make changes, fine tune it, tweak it. This ability comes from gaining knowledge and experience.

The week ending 17th August 2007– one of the most volatile weeks ever, one of the traders I recently interviewed banked nearly

3000 pips, yet he had more losing trades than winning trades. The most important thing is that you must be disciplined to follow your trading system and manage your risk – a case of cutting losses and letting profits run. One successful trader I recently interviewed trades GBPJPY and for the past 2 years has consistently averaged over £10,000 monthly profits, yet 50% of his trades are losing trades!

Does he have a "perfect System" giving him 100% wining trades? NO – But he follows his tested system with absolute discipline, and when the price deviates from the system he manages it and comes out but he also lets the winners run – Risk Management.

His system is very simple – what you see on the charts is just the price, support & resistance levels, a few relevant moving averages and just one indicator. His ability to simplify the system meant that he was able to eliminate a lot of unnecessary and complicated analysis thus not resulting into the paralysis of his brain!

I help traders become more successful – How? I teach simple stuff that works, it requires no complex strategies or rocket science, No analysis paralysis. Often many traders will buy complex charting packages and will attend each and every free seminar and read every book on offer. They will go through every type of indicator leading to analysis paralysis. Too much knowledge becomes overwhelming.

The Bindal FX system filters out all of the "noise" and focuses on simple methodology. We encourage members not to overload with lots of information whether analysis of charts, fundamental news, or listening to "gurus" – if you do listen to "gurus" than you must build a strong filtering system to weed out nonsense information. You have to cut out everything, except the information you need for your system.

Paralysis by Analysis is one of the most dangerous traps a trader can fall into. I have often seen charts sent to me having well over half a dozen indicators, which often conflict with one another, this an result in undermining confidence in the system and lead to a complete loss of trading discipline.

How to Deal With Analysis Paralysis

Mental paralysis is the result of having no idea of what to do or having too many options to choose from and when this occurs, a trader is unable to move forward to take action. You can use a few simple steps to prevent and move through analysis paralysis.

Get a Role Model – You don't need to reinvent the wheel. A role model and mentor are vital factors to consider having, as this can enable you to fast track your success. You can use what has been used by experts before and you can replicate it, use only that methodology that suits your trading mindset.

Know what you are analysing – If you do not understand what you are looking for you will never find it. It is also true that you will find what you are looking for. Your mind is a much better computer than any that man has ever constructed. All you have to do is give it the right program and you will get the right result.
Use a limited number of rules – ideally 5 or less, and avoid using highly correlated rules.

Give up on perfection – accept the fact that there does NOT exist nor will ever exist a "perfect" trading system, instead focus on a system that has a high probability of success with a sound risk management plan.

Focus Appropriately – You must concentrate and focus only on the small tasks at hand. Multi tasking can lead to divided attention leading to minimal progress. By placing all your attention on one or two key points of analysis will enable you to master the situation at hand early!

Analyse & back test – Look for patterns that repeatedly occur, for example the use of dynamic power of EMAs as support & resistance levels.

Assemble the trading system – Always look for confluence of indicators to execute a trade.

Tips on defeating Analysis Paralysis

Keep in mind that failure is often accelerated not by the decisions made, but by the failure to make those decisions at critical times such as getting in the trade at the right time, right price and exit strategies.

In Trading, analysis paralysis is a major concern. Begin with simple technical analysis and stick to simple rules.

Find a buddy – networking with successful traders can often help you in your trading, you can review your trading methodology and Plans with your "successful" trading buddy – this can provide a great boost against procrastination.

DECIDE – Get used to making decisions, it gets easier with practice, start with small decisions. It is those small steps that will enable you to achieve great success.

Gain momentum – regardless of where you are on your journey through life, momentum will make your ride easier and more effortless, and again this can be achieved by taking those small steps one at a time. Momentum and confidence is gained by seeing the successful outcome of those small steps.

SUMMARY & ACTION POINTS

1. DO NOT Procrastinate due to over analysis. Analysis without action is useless and will not achieve the results. Now that you have tips on how to overcome analysis paralysis, why don't you take that small step to enhance your life today? STOP THINKING and GO do it now!

2. CLARIFY in your own mind the questions you would like answered as a result of your analysis, that will help design a solution.

"All business sagacity reduces itself in the last analysis to judicious use of sabotage"

Thorstein Veblen

CHAPTER 4

KISS PRINCIPLE APPLIED

"Most great people have attained their greatest success just one step beyond their greatest failure."

Napoleon Hill

Having gone through the topics of the KISS principle and paralysis by over analysis, I would like you to observe the following charts taken over the four week period in July and August of 2007.

The charts are very simple, and do not have any indicators at all. The Currency pair covered on the chart is GBPUSD and includes the following:

Price
200 ema
610 ema (thick line)

With the KISS principle, all you are doing is focussing on Price action and the overall trend.

Chart 1 GBP 26th July to 31st July 2007

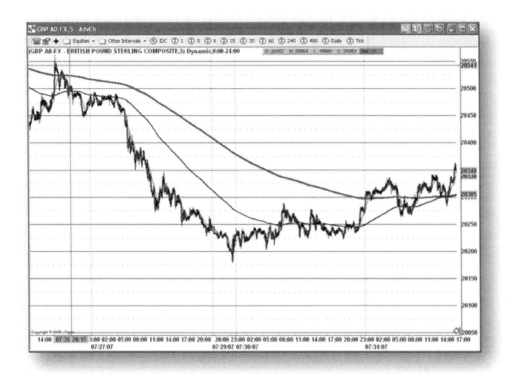

Chart source eSignal www.eSignal.com

Your Observations

Chart 2 GBP 30th July to 3rd August 2007

Chart source eSignal www.eSignal.com

Your Observations

Chart 3 EURJPY – 21st Jan 2008

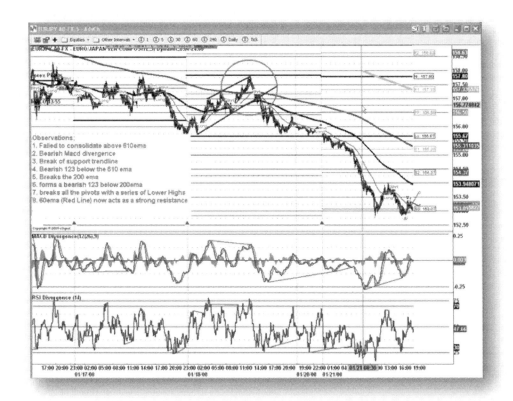

Chart source eSignal www.eSignal.com

Your Observations

A full list of observations already given to you, above. A very strong case of a short signal.

What is the main observation you make from the above chart? At this stage focusing simply on the price action and the emas.

Chart 4 GBP 2nd August to 7th August 2007

Chart source eSignal www.eSignal.com

Your Observations

Chart 5 GBP 6th August to 9th August 2007

Chart source eSignal www.eSignal.com

Your Observations

Chart 6 GBP 8th August to 9th August 2007

Chart source eSignal www.eSignal.com

Your Observations

Chart 7 GBP 9th August to 10th August 2007

Chart source eSignal www.eSignal.com

Your Observations

Chart 8 GBP 12th August to 15th August 2007

Chart source eSignal www.eSignal.com

Your Observations

Chart 9 GBP 14th August to 17th August 2007

Chart source eSignal www.eSignal.com

Your Observations

Chart 10 GBP 17th August to 22nd August 2007

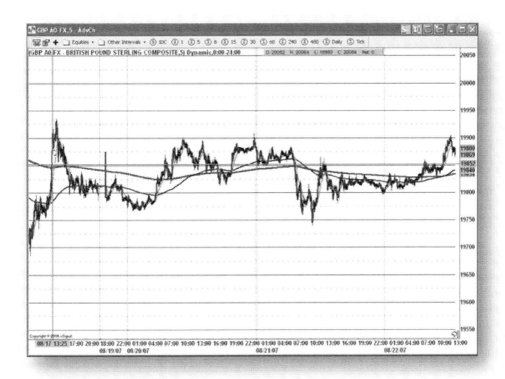

Chart source eSignal www.eSignal.com

Your Observations

Chart 11 GBP 22nd August to 24th August 2007

Chart source eSignal www.eSignal.com

Your Observations

SUMMARY & ACTION POINTS

1.) What were your observations? Be honest! Did it include any of the following?

- Price action on currency will trend most of the time, very rarely it will be sideways for a long time.

- Very clear 123 setups (to be covered in later chapters)

- EMAs acted as DYNAMIC support & resistance levels.

- When prices broke the 200 / 610ema **_followed by a 123_**, it offered a low risk, high probability trade.

- Focus on the price action – observe what it is doing. Is it creating higher highs and higher lows in an uptrend? Lower lows and lower highs in a downtrend? If so then use 123 setup for entry.

- Very simple! KISS Principle in action. No complex indicators.

CHAPTER 5

KNOW YOURSELF

"Know your enemy, know yourself, fight a hundred battles, and win a hundred battles."

Teachings of Hsun Wu

The above quote still holds true today in every aspect of life, be it a career, sports, politics or indeed trading. 95% of traders fail, but your actions and thoughts will determine whether you will succeed or fail, you are in control and you alone must take responsibility of your actions.

There are tremendous opportunities in the markets, it does not matter what Greenspan or Bernanke or Trichet says. It does not matter what economic policies a government adopts. All that matters is what actions YOU take that could make a difference between success and failure as a trader.

An average person spends the majority of their time listening to people who have not achieved much in life! – For example reporters, TV or radio personalities or even the pundits. If you want to achieve mastery then you need to listen to those people who have what you want. Find a role model and learn what they did.

The biggest opportunity to succeed in trading is right now, there is no limit to success available, however the reason one is likely to fail is because of mental scarcity not because of scarcity of opportunity. There is absolutely no limit to success. Firstly you have to accept that there is no limit to success and you have to have the confidence and belief in your ability to succeed – knowing yourself empowers you and success comes easily.

Once you know who you are, then you need to ascertain what you want – your desires and dreams. You now have a much better chance of succeeding.

Nine Steps For Getting To Know Yourself

1.) Spend quality time with yourself – Always start your day positively and with a winning attitude. Listen to motivational tapes, focus on good and positive thoughts in life, and visualize success. More importantly enjoy and have fun, do not be a workaholic, balance your life with work and pleasure.

2.) What do you want? – In order to create the life you want, it is very important to know what's really important to you, what are you most passionate about? Once you have a strong passion, you will find a strong enough reason why you want it, and it will overpower any obstacles standing in your way. With a strong enough reason, the motivation to take action will naturally come to you.

3.) Keep a Journal – Your mind is your inbox, and we need to clean it up, and one of the ways to do this is to keep a journal, in which you jot down the major occurrences each day, paying particular attention to emotion specific details. If there was an event that particularly bothered you, write it down. After writing it down, it may be that you look at it differently, if not then ask an empowering question as to how could you have handled it better? What steps can you take to ensure that the experience is not repeated? Of course you will also have many positive things to write down, use this success to your advantage – you can replicate this achievement over and over.

4.) Get Help – Sometimes you need an expert to help you move forward, and that could be a teacher, a role model or a mentor. Before you seek out a mentor you must have a clear focus of where you are now, and where you want to be. A mentoring relationship is a transfer of skills; a mentor is someone who will help you grow in areas that are most important to you.

5.) Get a Buddy – Find a buddy who has already begun a journey of self-awareness and inner healing. Trading can be very lonely, so have the right company to mutually guide each other by sharing your experiences.

6.) Discover your blind spots - Do you know what your weaknesses are? Once you can identify what these blind spots are you can go about correcting them, you will then achieve success much faster.

7.) Personal Development – Develop yourself on an ongoing basis and you can achieve extraordinary results! Personal development techniques can help you achieve results by gaining ability to set the plans that you desire, enabling you to gain momentum in achieving your goals. It will also help you to understand what makes you tick. It will enable you to develop skills on how to react to market volatility, on how to handle such emotions as the fear of loss or greed.

8.) Developing capacity to take risks and accept challenges - Once you have applied all the above points of keeping a journal, setting goals, getting a buddy etc, now is the time to take action. You now need to put in practice all your new found knowledge and make it work for you, and that is when the true test will come. You now have to take massive action to accomplish your goals, it is now necessary to take a plunge and move forward, at the same time balance it with caution, with your golden rule of No Signal – No Trade!

9.) Have Fun – You must have a life after work. Spending quality time with family and friends socializing and relaxing. There are many things that you can do to enjoy and have fun. You can turn to sports, have hobbies, travel, nature, and singing – overall just relax and have fun. It is important that you are with people you like, who inspire and encourage you to be a better person. You now have the success that you desired, so it is time to have fun and enjoy that success.

SUMMARY & ACTION POINTS

1.) Name three things that you like about yourself?

2.) What are your hopes for the future?

3.) What inspires you?

4.) What your special talents?

5.) What are your Core Values?

6.) What is the thing you are most proud of accomplishing in your life so far?

7.) What skills do you need to develop and why?

8.) What is your most important goal right now and why?

9.) Why MUST you absolutely achieve this goal?

10.)   What brings out the best in you?

"What lies behind us and what lies before us are tiny matters compared to what lies within us"

Oliver Wendell

YOUR GOALS

GOALS:

Dreams With a Deadline

Conceive Believe Achieve

First say to yourself what you would be;
And then do what you have to do.

CHAPTER 6

GOALS

"Dreams are a dime a dozen...... it's their execution that counts."

Theodore Roosevelt

Knowledge helps you reach your destination – provided you know what the destination is.

From Bhagavad Gita

Acharya Drona was an ancient Hindu sage who taught his disciples the art of archery, one day he arranged a test to decide the best archer amongst all.

A wooden bird was put on a branch of a tree, it was partly hidden by the leaves and an artificial eye was painted on the wooden bird. He asked all the disciples that he wanted them to shoot at the target, which was the eye. Drona asked all the disciples what they saw. The disciples came with various answers such as the people, the leaves, the clouds, the sky, the tree, the bird. Each of the disciples were asked to step aside, as the Sage felt that they had poor concentration and therefore would miss the target.

Lastly, it was the turn of Arjuna, who readied himself to hit the target. The Sage asked Arjuna the same question, "Tell me what is being observed by you?"

Arjuna replied " At this point in time ONLY the eye of the bird is visible to me" When asked by the sage whether he was able to see the bird, the tree, the sky etc, Arjuna replied that he only saw the eye of the bird.

Drona was pleased with Arjuna's immense concentration and correct approach. The sage asked Arjuna to shoot. The Arrow hit the target!

Lack of focus stops you achieving your targets. Peak performers realize this truth and TAKE ACTION accordingly – You too can begin right away, if you choose to focus and concentrate, a skill that can be learned.

Tip – You can create unlimited potential by positive focus and concentration. Eastern teachings & philosophy can often be a trader's greatest asset. Yoga, meditation and Pranayama can assist with improving your power of focus and concentration.

Why are Goals important?

Majority of traders fail because;

- They do not know what they are looking to achieve.
- They do not have a goal or a target set.
- They do not have a big enough reason why they need the success.
- They do not have the tools, the system and methodology.

If you do not have a Plan you will just drift away without any direction whatsoever. You have no control! By setting goals and having an action plan enables you to become more focused and this will help to speed your progress. Therefore it is absolutely essential to have trading goals. One of the best acronyms I have seen is to set a "SMART" goal

S – SPECIFIC. Goals must be specific and you must define exactly what you want e.g. I will consistently make 150 pips per week within 6 months.

M – MEASURABLE. Your goals must be measurable, this will enable you to monitor the progress and give you feedback if you are on track.

A – ACHIEVABLE. Your goals must be ambitious and challenging, but they must be attainable. You have to have the belief that you can achieve your goals. There must not be any doubts whatsoever.

R – REALISTIC. If your goal is to make 1000 pips next month, when you have never achieved 100 pips ever, then you are being unrealistic. You must make those small steps towards achieving that ultimate target of a 1000 pips.

T – TIME. You must set a deadline within which to achieve your goals.

Getting what you want does not always come easy, to achieve your goals you have to work very hard at it, and trading is no different. This requires dedication, perseverance and monitoring your performance.

You may have the greatest passion to succeed as a trader, you can be totally dedicated, and you can be absolutely enthusiastic about trading. These positive emotions would be totally useless and meaningless if you did not have a target to aim for. Goals give you a sense of direction.

Goal Setting – Simple formula

Once you follow the SMART principle, your goals can be achieved, anything you want you can accomplish, it is impossible for you to fail, if you follow these SMART principles.

In addition you can use the following SUCCESS FORMULA for your goals to be achieved;

DECIDE what you want. In order to get what you want you have to decide what you want. Once you decide what you want the brain will figure out how to get it. Your mind and the universe will step in.

CREATE A PLAN. Be sure to write down your plan, do not just keep it in your mind, and always remember "So as it is written, so shall it be done" If you do not know how to create a plan, find someone to help you.

DEADLINE. A goal without a deadline never gets completed. A deadline motivates you to develop a plan of action in order to achieve the goal.

ACTION. For you to succeed in achieving your goals, what matters is the action you take, your life will only change if you decide to take action to change it.

FOLLOW THROUGH. Lack of follow through can be deadly, one way to build momentum is to do at least 3 things everyday toward achieving your goal. Often having a buddy or a mentor can help you push towards taking this action.

READ. You must read your goals at least 3 times a day, this will enable you to stay focused.

POSITIVE THINKING. The positive mental attitude will drive the subconscious mind to expect successful outcome. This will in some way assist in removing fear and also provide will power and strength.

REVIEW. It is very important to find out if you are on track with your plans, if not you can take early action to make the necessary changes. Regular reviews must happen.

VISUALISE. The daily practice of visualizing your goals being achieved can accelerate your progress, because it activates your creative subconscious mind to start generating ideas and also recognizes what resources are needed. It further activates the law of attraction, thereby drawing into your life all the people and resources that you will need in order to achieve success. Visualization will also build motivation.

BELIEF. Napoleon Hill said, "Whatever the mind can conceive and believe, it can achieve." Act as though you have achieved it.

HAVE FUN. Do what you love and start enjoying what you do, having this strong passion can motivate you and build the momentum.

CELEBRATE. Whenever you achieve small success, you are winning the battles, you must enjoy and celebrate the success, and this will keep the momentum going and enable you to ultimately win the war.

If you can set SMART goals, have a belief in your goals, and then take massive action to achieve those goals, then you can do incredible things! – dreams can come true.

Get a Life – Create a work-life balance

All work and no play makes you a dull guy – a dull trader will end up losing, so spice up your life! Not having an active life after work can add to stress, irritation, depression, anxiousness and not to mention health and relationship problems – this may result into a losing trader.

Look at some of the wealthiest people ever, what happened to their lives;

- Jesse Livermore, the greatest trader committed suicide.
- Arthur Cutton, one of the greatest commodity traders died insolvent.
- Charles Schwab, President of a largest steel company died bankrupt.
- Ivar Kruger, head of a greatest monopoly committed suicide.

The list is endless........... These men learnt the art of making money, but failed to learn how to learn to live a "rich life". Money and success are important to all in a civilized society, to think that money is not important is absurd but you need to enjoy life and the money that has been earned.

Work hard and play hard – that is life! You should learn to live your life to the fullest.

SUMMARY & ACTION POINTS

1.) Define Success and what it means to you?

2.) What is your dream?

3.) Why is it your dream?

4.) What does it mean to you to achieve your dreams?

5.) What PLANS have you made to achieve your goals?

6.) What skills you need to acquire?

7.) What actions you intend to take in the direction of your goal?

8.) How would you feel when your dream is achieved?

CHAPTER 7
BELIEF

"Men often become what they believe themselves to be. If I believe I cannot do something, It makes me incapable of doing it. But when I believe I can, I acquire the ability to do it even if I didn't have it in the beginning".

Mahatma Gandhi

Believe in yourself, you are worth it and you have the ability to do the incredible! You have unlimited potential within you. Belief in yourself is the most important secret to your trading success. How much faith and belief you have in your trading plan will control your trading performance. I am of the belief that YOU are the GURU, and the GURU is within you, trading mastery is within you.

How long have you been trading? 1 year?, 5 years?, 10 years? Right now think about your trading performance to date, how have you performed? What is your cumulative profit or loss to date? Write it down on a blank piece of paper – be totally honest with yourself. You can estimate it, if you have not kept records. Just write it down! Don't skip this exercise.

How do you feel about your performance? Are you happy or unhappy about it? No doubt you don't want to be where you are, you want to achieve mastery, and you want to join the 5% club. What you have achieved to date is your past, you have suffered and survived and experience may transform your future.

What is a belief?

Belief is the psychological state in which the individual has a feeling of certainty about the outcome. If you say that you believe that your trade will be a winner, it means that you feel certain that it will be a winning trade. The sense of certainty gives you the confidence and therefore removes the fear from your decision making thus allowing your brain and the subconscious mind to tap into resources – Our brain can achieve incredible results.

You may have a great trading system but a weak belief in your system. You trading system fires a signal, you follow it and pull the trigger. If you do not have the belief in the system, then as soon as the trade were to go against you, you would panic and bail out, just as you close your trade, the markets reverse and go in the direction of your trade but without you on board. The trader in this case did not have the belief and confidence in the system, else he would have given the trade a chance to either work for or against him. Unless you start to believe in your trading system you are destined to fail!

How can you develop belief?

Testing - One of the ways that you can gain confidence and belief in your trading system is to have had some experience to support the method, and that will strengthen your belief. Have a written step by step plan of what conditions need to be met before you execute a trade, you need to test it in a "live" trading environment – not just back testing. You have to trade it initially using a demo account. Any successful trading will now give you a reference point to support your system. One trader I had recently coached used the Bindal FX system to trade live on a demo account. He only moved to a real money trading account after achieving a cumulative target of a 1000 pips. He has not looked back and has moved on from strength to strength and has truly made Forex mastery – a child's play!

Imagination is the ability to form mental pictures in your mind, following your system and achieving success at the same time creating a tremendous amount of emotional intensity then repeating this exercise at regular intervals. One of my successful trading graduates wanted to master trading divergence setups, he spent up to 30 minutes everyday meditating on successful divergence trading, constantly rehearsing trading the setups in his mind - the visualization was so real that he saw himself taking the trades which met his criteria. Not only did this reinforce his confidence, but he was absolutely certain of success. Presently, he is averaging over 2000 pips per month, and he is still continuing with this exercise. It certainty does carry power!

"If my mind can Conceive it, my heart can Believe it, I know I can Achieve it"

Jesse Jackson

If you develop an absolute sense of certainty that you will succeed as a trader, that the trade you are about to take will be a winner, and you act and behave as if it was true, you can eventually be a master trader. What you don't want to do is to focus on failure or a losing trade, whatever you focus on will manifest. If you focus on fear and loss, then no matter how powerful a system you have, you are likely to lose!

So focus on winning, focus on the profit and focus on the success.

Avoid a destructive mindset – If you believe that achieving success as a trader is very difficult, you will fail because your fears will manifest. If after doing all the analysis on a trade, and when executing a trade, your focus is on the loss and not the profit, your emotions of a destructive mindset will take over, and it is likely that you will lose the trade.

Experience a positive mindset – A positive mindset is the foundation for success. Follow your plan, have confidence in your plan and when executing the trade, do it in a relaxed and happy frame of mind, expecting a profit and nothing else! Experience the feeling of success!

Personal Development – No matter at what stage of life you may be at, you must always strive to get better and constantly improve the quality of your life. You must challenge yourself and always strive to move out of your comfort zone. Everyday you must improve yourself in some way.

"Men often become what they believe themselves to be. If I believe I cannot do something, it makes me incapable of doing it. But when i believe I can, then I acquire the ability to do it even if I didn't have it in the beginning"

Mahatma Gandhi

SUMMARY & ACTION POINTS

1.) Belief is a feeling of certainty.

2.) Write 10 things you believe about you. Be open and be honest with you, as you need to also include negative beliefs so that you can start to address them.

3.) List all the personal qualities that you require to achieve forex mastery?

4.) Select your best trading strategy, one that you like to trade and are familiar with. Visualise step by step you pulling the trigger as per your trading plan, and then see yourself managing the trade.

5.) Taking incremental profits and letting the profits run. See yourself closing the trade when the signal reverses.

6.) Why are you NOT achieving your true potential, is it because some limiting beliefs are holding you back? If so, it is time to say goodbye to them and fill the vacuum with new empowering beliefs.

CHAPTER 8

POWER OF THOUGHTS

"Every thought is a seed, if your thoughts are focused on a fear of a loss, then don't expect a profit".

Jayendra Lakhani

The thoughts that pass through your mind are responsible for everything that happens in your life. Thoughts are one of the most powerful emotions that you have and if you use them positively, they can transform your life.

Success is not dependant on luck, success in any field is determined by the actions that you take, and the thoughts you have will determine what actions you take. Thoughts will make you take actions on your desires and dreams thereby enabling you to achieve goals.

So what must you do? You must fill your mind with positive and inspirational material and avoid any thoughts that will kill your dreams – Doubt, fear and negative thinking. Change your thinking and you will end up having a prosperous life!

Look at what some of the brightest minds had to say about the power of thought;

"All action results from a thought, so it is thoughts that matter"

Sai Baba

"All that we are is the result of what we have thought"

Buddha

"Unless our good thoughts are translated into action, we will be like trees that bear no fruit"

Swami Ramdas

"Drag your thoughts away from the fear of a loss, these negative emotions have tremendous power and it will break you"

Jayendra Lakhani

"The winning trader will always focus his thoughts in terms of I am, and I can – these positive thoughts will manifest"

Jayendra Lakhani

If you think in negative terms before you execute a trade, if your focus is on a loss or fear, then it is likely that you will lose from the trade taken. If on the other hand, once your system has generated a signal, you take appropriate action with full confidence of a winning trade. You are expecting nothing but a profit, the probability is much higher that you will get a profitable trade. We can be a winner, but the choice is within us.

Thoughts determine our choices and the actions that we take. Thoughts are an activity of your mind and you can choose your thoughts. Emotions follow thoughts. Negative thoughts can destroy you as you will not be able to see any opportunities that exist. Positive thoughts stimulate activity, assisting in transforming your life. Positive thought relaxes your thinking process therefore new ideas will also come in your mind. Positive thoughts will enhance the body's immune system and can lead to a healthy life.

Invest in your mind

To achieve consistent success, you must always challenge yourself and constantly strive to do better and better, to move out of your comfort zone. To do this you have to develop, grow and build yourself through personal development. To change your thinking you have to change what goes in your mind. Read powerful books that will motivate you, listen to motivational audio tapes or go to a course on personal development. Your mind will now be programmed to achieve success.

If you think you will lose, you will lose
If you like to win but think you can't, you won't win
The trader who wins is the trader who thinks he is the winner

You can do it!

You can Conceive it!

You can achieve it!

You can believe it!

You can receive it!

Great thoughts do great things!

You can do it! You can do it!

YES I CAN! – Never ever doubt your ability. Miracles can happen when you believe in your ability. Your dreams can become reality if you change your thinking. Change your thought process with tremendous intensity to the point where you totally believe that you can simply not fail.

"Your thoughts can lead you to actions".

SUMMARY & ACTION POINTS

1.) Mind Power – It is possible to train and strengthen the mind, as it is your thoughts that will influence your behaviour, attitude and your actions.

2.) Thoughts become things.

3.) Your mind is creative, for success you have tap on to this power to your advantage.

4.) Visualise the perfect scene of what goals /desires you wish to achieve.

5.) Empowering thoughts are benefits you and also the mankind by improving the vibrations.

6.) Evil thoughts harm YOU and also the mankind by creating the negative vibrations.

7.) Powerful thoughts inspire us thus creating vision and you are able to tap into the higher consciousness.

8.) How do you know if the thought is powerful? – Your feelings and emotions will tell you. You will feel good and will be at peace.

CHAPTER 9

POWER OF QUESTIONS

"Questions focus our thinking. Ask empowering questions like: What's good about this? What's not perfect about it yet? What am I going to do next time? How can I do this and have fun doing it?"

Charles Connolly

Questions have great power, the direction of your life depends on the quality of questions that you ask When a trader gets stopped out and then precisely at that moment, the market turns, he asks "Why does this always happen to me?"

What response will your mind give you on the above question? Nothing! It would create more frustration leading to more failure. Quality questions can create success. How about if the trader asked the following questions;

"What can I do about this, so that I can achieve consistent profit in my trades?"

"What can I learn from this stopped out trade?"

"In what ways is my current trading system perfect?"

"How long will it take me to achieve success as a trader?"

"When should I review my trading plan?"

"How can I keep myself motivated in order to ensure trading success?"

"How can I succeed and take action, whilst many fear failure?"

"How can I turn this around?"

By asking these quality empowering questions, your brain will come with solutions. Our brain can think for itself and is the most powerful computer. Nothing that mankind has created has even come close to the complexity of the human brain. So the quickest way to change a focus is to ask an empowering question. Ask and you shall receive.

These questions require POSITIVE answers that enable you to take the necessary action to learn and to grow.

Questions Determine Thoughts

I experienced the 1987 crash, I experienced the market bear move during the Iraqi war, I experienced the market meltdown during the Monica Lewinsky affair, I experienced the Nasdaq meltdown in 2000 and many more market crashes. Recently I saw the GBPJPY meltdown in August 2007, a move of 3000 pips. I not only survived these meltdowns, but overall made many successful trades during these periods.

How did I do it? When things went wrong I asked better questions rather then get frustrated about a "past" event. If I needed to become a consistent winner, I needed to ask questions that enabled me to focus on the task at hand, and therefore I was also changing the way I thought.

If you ask better questions, you get better answers. Quality questions will create a quality life. Quality questions will lead to a good trading plan, to a good trading methodology.

Quality questions will determine the way you trade, and your success will depend on those questions. If you are fearful of a loss, it is often this fear that keeps you away from taking necessary action. For example when the system gives a valid trading signal, you are unable to take the trade or it could be this fear to bail out as soon as you have a small loss only to see the market reverse in the direction of your trade. It is also this fear that forces you to close a winning trade early and snatch a profit.

The questions that you ask will determine your focus, it will determine your thoughts and therefore the actions that you take.

Peak Performance Questions

Total commitment by you will ensure reaching the ultimate in your performance as a trader. A peak performer will ask powerful questions and then develop powerful metal images of the answers. This will motivate them to take massive action to achieve the desired results. The peak performer will visualize the result he wants and what actions he needs to take.

You must ask yourself powerful questions that will help you stay focused and therefore get better results;

Q.) What are my highest value activities? – What are the activities that bring value and effectiveness in your life? Discovering yourself will give you a sense of direction or purpose.

Q.) What is my Key Performance Area (KPA) – KPA's are one of the most important tools for performance management. What are your SMART goals? It enables you to review and measure the performance level. Defining KPA's can motivate you thus enabling you to focus on achieving the results.

Q.) Why am I trading? – what is your purpose in trading the markets? Do you enjoy trading? Do you have a passion? What do you intend to achieve?

Q.) What actions do I need to take to make a real difference to my life as a trader?

Q.) Currently what is the most valuable use of my time? This can be a very challenging exercise enabling you to focus single minded on your KPA's – a key to high performance.

"Quality questions create a quality life, Successful people ask better questions, and as a result, they get better answers."

Anthony Robbins

SUMMARY & ACTION POINTS

1.) Questions have great power. One right question asked at the right time can shape your destiny.

2.) Reframe your questions to create inspiration – from negative to positive, i.e. why is this happening to me? Into > What can I lean from this?

3.) Ask a question that provokes thought.

4.) Ask yourself 25 Thought provoking questions, and than go about answering them with absolute honesty.

5.) *"If I had an hour to solve a problem and my life depended on the solution, I would spend the first 55 minutes determining the proper question to ask, for once I know the proper question; I could solve the problem in less than five minutes."* —Albert Einstein

CHAPTER 10 – SMALL STEPS

"Whoever wants to reach a distant goal must take small steps."

Helmut Schmidt

The majority of goals set, never get accomplished. Research shows that 95% of New Year's resolutions are never achieved. Do you need to make significant changes in your life? Change in your life can happen in an instant, it happens the moment you decide to take that small step towards achieving a goal.

Often we think that achieving your dreams are beyond our grasp, and you really need to be superhuman to achieve the incredible. We are all incredible and we can all achieve the incredible things in life. Most changes are a result of taking micro-actions each day, and that will make a difference to your life. If you can truly make a commitment to be different at the end of the month, these small changes will positively impact your life. The first step may be so small, yet those small steps lead to great rewards.

Small steps are key to success in trading. If your goal is to earn a thousand pips per month, you cannot achieve this immediately. You have got to start off very small. Your ultimate goal may be 1000 pips, but each month's goal should be a small improvement over the previous month. You are constantly challenging yourself.

Your Defining Moment

At some point in life, you will come across life changing experiences, or indeed a series of events in your lifetime that will change the course of YOUR history. I call those experiences your defining moments.

All you need is just one moment in your life that defines the direction of your life and that will determine your destiny. The defining moment is when it becomes clear and obvious what you need to do. You experience a mental shift and have taken a DECISION. From this point onwards, all you need is to carry out small steps to make that change a reality.

When was your defining moment? If you haven't got one then make it NOW – Today. Make a commitment and make a decision to change your life forever.

For Gandhi, the defining moment was on a train journey in South Africa, that was the start of the end of the Great British Empire. For Rosa Parks, It was on a bus when she refused to give up her seat, her defining moment altered the course of American history. For Mother Teresa, the defining moment was to devote her life to serve the needy.

Each of these figures made a DECISION to change and make a contribution beyond themselves. They set their goal, they committed and they took ACTION.

YOU too have the ability to create your defining moment, Don't just sit there – CREATE your defining moment and then Live Your Dreams. We all have defining moments, but many of us just simply back off from these defining moments, many fail to take action because they are uncomfortable when all it takes is one small step to change your life. It is your ACTION that makes the difference. Defining moments! Those moments can shape your future.

Recognise Your Defining Moment

One's defining moment can be a result of procrastination, life is just flowing without any purpose, and then one says "enough is enough". You now want to change, take action and succeed.

What steps can you take to recognize your defining moment?

Understand and know the Symptoms;

Dissatisfied with status quo, you want more!
You have vast potential but have not achieved it.
Procrastination – you have the ability but choose not to take action.

Lack of Consistency

1.) Know yourself and be honest – you need to sit back and analyse the experience and put your thoughts on paper.

2.) Take Massive Action - Don't let this moment pass without taking action. At this point you have a clear idea of your defining moment. Be totally focused on it.

3.) Create a plan of action and make the change. Implement your plan.

Defining moments are combinations of thoughts and actions that shape our future, they include decisions that shape our tomorrow. If you think you can't, you won't. If you think you can, there's a good chance you will.

SUMMARY & ACTION POINTS

1.) Have you been putting off taking action on a goal? Come up with one small step that you can take within the next 24 hours – and JUST DO IT!

2.) What is your defining moment NOW? What action will you take?

3.) Write down three of your EXPERIENCES that made a strong impression on you, describe it in a paragraph.

4.) What small steps will you take to achieve the change?

5.) To achieve, you have to DECIDE to make a change, set a GOAL, COMMIT and take ACTION.

6.) Read about some real life defining moments for inspiration.

CHAPTER 11

MASTER TRADERS THINK & ACT DIFFERENTLY

"Winners don't do different things.... They do things differently."

Shiv Khera

The above quote by Shiv Khera says it all – it clearly differentiates between the actions of winners and losers, and trading is no different. Have you ever wondered why so many traders fail miserably at trading? I could give 10 traders a similar trading system yet they will all come with different results. In fact you will have more losers then winners!

What do winners do to achieve great success? think about it! Nothing special or great which YOU cannot do, they just do things in a different way, a different style to achieve their dreams and desires.

Trading need not be difficult. It can truly be a childs play. There is no rocket science, there is no secret and indeed there is no forex code to crack. The secret to trading mastery is to think and act differently than the majority and as a result perform better.

What Do Master Traders Do Things Differently?

Fear - They recognize their fears and are willing to take necessary actions that most traders will not. Master traders focus on their equity preservation and will ensure that they cut the losses and let the winners run.

Ego – Everyone likes to be a winning trader. However trading success is achieved by being ruthlessly disciplined in following your trading plans. You must learn to trade without ego getting in the way. Ego can ruin your trading success, the best example being when Nick Leeson brought down the Barings Bank. The lesson is if you are wrong get out! Traders who have ego's get killed. They think they are smarter than the market and that they are right and the market is wrong. A trader with an ego will never achieve long term success. Learn to respect the market.

Greed – Greed is necessary, for it is the greed that drives the markets and provides the motivation. But if you lose the balance then greed is what causes most traders to stay in a trade for too long or indeed to take on a trade when there was no signal. You do not need to take every possible trade. If you miss a move then there is no need to chase the market if your trading system has not fired a signal.

Hype - Master traders do not get caught up in the hype when markets make highs or when the market makes lows. Analysts and market gurus are quick to talk of boom times during the highs, and the doom and gloom during the market lows. Most of these so called gurus are wrong, so don't get caught up in this! Focus on charts and technical analysis and particularly your trading plan. You must have belief and confidence in your plan.

Trade the Plan – Master traders trade a proven and tested system and follow it ruthlessly. Golden Rule – No Signal No Trade!

Trading Journal – I have often mentioned that YOU are your biggest mentor, and the trading journal is one such tool which can provide you with immense potential to improve. Keeping a Journal may be tedious and cumbersome, but it can dramatically improve results, as it adds discipline in your trading thought process.

Can You Expect Different Results From The Same Effort?

You have to realize that if you want different results you will have to take different actions and also have different thoughts! – Yes, fill your mind with confident and positive thoughts. You must change and constantly challenge yourself. In fact you should challenge yourself daily. You can try to do one thing differently every day that would stretch you. The idea is to do one simple thing every day that not only furthers your trading success or personal life but is also something that will challenge you. Replacing bad habits with good ones can be a long and arduous task, but to make a change, you must challenge yourself to do things differently and at the same time have fun!

The Rules

- Set yourself a period in which you intend to make a change. Make a list of "New Challenges" that you intend to undertake.

- Make it fun – how many new challenges can you undertake?

- Monitor progress, how do you feel when new challenges are being achieved?

- Get a buddy to motivate you and to push you.

- Follow the challenge for at least 30 days.

- 30 days of new action can form a new habit.

Examples of new challenges or activity that you can do;

- A record of all your trades with reasons why you took the trade – set up a trading journal.

- Never trade without a stop.

- Meditate and visualize daily on your trading methodology, and see yourself achieving success.

- Exercise everyday.

- Listen to trading tutorials daily.

- Reading motivational and inspirational books.

- Regular stretches throughout the day.

- Have a life outside trading – an active social life.

- Listen to uplifting music.

The Results

After a 30 day challenge, you will have had great fun, the new activity should now form a habit and you will now find it difficult not to follow.

What are you going to do to challenge yourself today?

"Success is the old ABS – Ability, breaks, and courage"
Charles Luckman.

SUMMARY & ACTION POINTS

1.) List 10 things that you could do differently to succeed as a trader.

2.) What will be your personal challenge for today? Review it at the end of the day, did you achieve the result?

3.) What will be your personal challenge for the week? Review it at the end of the week, did you achieve the result?

4.) Challenge yourself daily – Do one thing differently and have fun.

CHAPTER 12

DISCIPLINE, MENTAL SKILL & TRADING PSYCHOLOGY

"It was character that got us out of bed, commitment that moved us into action, and discipline that enabled us to follow through."

Zig Ziglar

Are you searching for answers to become a master trader? Or are you still trying to be a profitable trader? Trading is not easy as most people think, why is it that out of all who try, over 90% fail?

My trading experience expands 2 decades, and also being a trading mentor I have also interviewed many traders, many of them have struggled to earn any profits after so many years of trading and yet they continue to fund their trading accounts.
Most traders do not realize that successful trading comes from a belief and confidence within oneself. It's an attitude! It's thinking like a winner. It's trading to win, not trading to lose. The fact is, trading, as all of you should know, is a zero sum game. You either

are a winner or a loser. Why does a trader let his loss accumulate? Why does a trader snatch a profit and not let it run? When you are wrong, why don't you admit it? All these answers come from within. It's trading psychology not technical knowledge. For anyone preparing a trading plan, the first thing you must do is to get to know yourself. This may seem silly, but 95% of trading plans that I have seen do not cover this important aspect.

Then the question arises, "why do a few win whilst most don't?"

First, think about this. Every trader has access to the same tools, the same research, the same charts, the same quotes, the same proven trading methods etc.

So, why is it that, with everybody having access to the same stuff, only a few make consistent profits over time?

Well, it's clear that the common denominator is the PERSON. Yes, YOU!

So, if somebody asked me to list the BIG THREE mental / emotional characteristics that define the majority of successful FOREX traders, I would list:

Discipline & Passion
Confidence & Courage
Patience & Persistence

One who has a great trading methodology and system, but is weak on psychology is likely to fail. Whereas someone with a mediocre trading system, but strong discipline with mental & psychology skills is likely to be on a winning side. One trader I recently interviewed had no clue about MACD, or Stochastic or RSIs or Elliott Wave. He has a very simple system of trading the breakout on triangles and trend lines – that's all he does, and consistently produces over 700 pips profit trading Forex. He has a simple system, a set of rules, sets achievable and realistic goals – and all he does is follow these simple rules! – No rocket science.

Recently one trader told me "I have read many good books by some of the great authors in the industry, however, after reading those I was still trying to find the 'secret' to trading successfully and was not sure about my system. I realised that the 'secret' to successful trading is that there is no secret!   I've also developed a system from very effective strategies that suit my psychology and my style, and more importantly I have devised a Trading Plan".

Discipline & Passion

Discipline

In my view discipline is the most important psychological factor that determines your success as a trader. The successful trader is a disciplined trader, who ruthlessly follows his trading plan. Discipline means controlling impulses and controlling emotions. Lack of discipline is probably the major reason why most traders fail. Majority of traders are not disciplined in their approach, else they would not be failing. These failed traders simply hate to hear the word Discipline! As Jack Schwager points out in his book, 'The New Market Wizards', "Discipline was probably the most frequent word used by the exceptional traders that I interviewed.

Discipline allows you to more effectively plan your work (trades) and work (trade) your plan. Discipline – "Habit of Obedience" – yes the keyword being habit, i.e. Have a Trading Plan and make a habit of following it.

The golden rule should be No Signal – No Trade.

The key to trading success is:

KISS principle trading system + Disciplined action = Trading success.

Learning about trading is very easy, but many traders do not have a strong mental fitness to succeed. To succeed in trading, create a simple yet powerful winning strategy, fully understand it, have confidence in the system, have full belief that the system works and trade with discipline. Sounds simple, yet most traders will continue to look for a secret or holy grail, but refuse to look within.

Components of trading discipline that I believe are essential if you are to succeed in trading;

Personal Development – You must always strive to get better at what you do and continually challenge yourself. Never rest on your past success and never accept that you have peaked. There is always room for improvement and your skills must be enhanced continually.

Golden Rules – You must have at least 10 trading rules that you will follow religiously. For example my number one Golden Rule is No Signal – No Trade. I will simply not trade without a signal. I must have a good enough reason why I must trade.

Patience – A disciplined trader has patience to let the trades either work for him or work against him. He will not panic at a loss, if he followed his system. Equally he will not snatch his profits, when there is more on the table, he will follow the trend. He is largely immune from panic and does not let hype or euphoria cloud his judgement.

Trading Plan – A disciplined trader will NOT trade without a plan and will develop a unique trading plan based on his psychology and style of trading. He will compare performance with his trading plan.

Feedback – A trader loses his edge as soon as he breaks his trading rules. Over a long term it could bring failure to the trader. Based on this immediate feedback the trader may want to get back to his rules and follow them.

Passion

"Nothing great in this world has ever been accomplished without passion"

Hebbel quotes

We may spend a third of our life working, so you deserve to feel fulfilled in what you do, you do it because you love to do it! – Yes the monetary rewards are the by-product of your success in doing things you love to do.

How can you be naturally successful at something, continue to fine-tune your trading skills, seek the services of a mentor, and stomach the ups and downs of the business. Do you know why you are trading? As Michael Jordan once said, "If you have a love for the game, your talent will eventually catch up to you." So if you do not have the love for trading, will you succeed?

No matter how difficult a situation can be or whatever challenges you face, having that burning passion and an excitement for the job that you do, can turn any obstacle into a tremendous opportunity.

So how can you become passionate about trading? Firstly you must enjoy what you do and then you must know what you want and why you want it? This in turn will create a deep desire and a passion to achieve your goals. You are inspired to take action because of the passion you have, the action you take will manifest your vision and this leads to success!

Find your purpose and you will find your passion! Find your passion and you will have your vision! You can begin by defining your vision and creating your own trading mission statement. Find some quiet moment to brainstorm and develop a statement of who you want to be.

Here are a few examples of what a mission statement could be for you.

To earn a $1 million from trading.
To set up a hedge fund or become a money manager.
To setup a charity from trading profits.

Example Mission Statements

Nike's Corporate Mission statement
"To bring inspiration and innovation to every athlete in the world"

Microsoft's corporate mission statement
"To enable people and business throughout the world to realize their full potential"

Bindal FX Mission Statement
"To create a community of successful Forex traders"

Having a mission statement will enable you to focus on your goals and how you can achieve them. It will enable you to take massive action!

<u>Confidence & Courage</u>

If you do not have confidence in your trading capability you are already defeated. With confidence you have already achieved success. There is no courage without confidence, and half the battle is in the belief that you are capable of achieving success.

One of the basic traits of successful traders is that they believe in themselves first. They have the confidence and courage to stick with their plan, not stray from their rules, go against the crowd if need be, and visualize success in their mind.

What does every successful TRADER have in common? From the book, 'Poker, Sex and Dying': "Poker is an explosive game combining money, ego, and emotions. It is not enough to know, have information, and insight regarding your opponent (the markets), you must know of yourself." Therefore within your trading plan, you must have a section about YOU – get to know yourself.

In the early days of my trading career, I had faced many a situation where I "knew" exactly where the price was going, had a trading plan, but failed to follow it. Of course, greed, fear, and our other emotions stood in our way. When you let this happen to you...all your knowledge, planning and information quickly becomes useless.

In other words, no matter how good you are at analysing the market, if you don't have confidence, all you're really doing is repeatedly creating experiences to which you will respond with similar frustration and anxiety.

Many traders are after an instant fix, looking for the holy grail or a secret which does not exist. Recently I saw an advert with a caption "Trade like a pro in 30 minutes". If only it was that easy, then everyone would be a winner, but in reality that is not the case. The real secret is following these simple steps, and you will achieve that confidence that you need to succeed!

How Do You Achieve Confidence?

Make a Decision – The most important thing is to decide what you want, and decide how you will achieve it. It does not have to be a huge goal, but start with something easy and simple. Take small steps and gradually challenge yourself every day. Get a big enough reason why you must absolutely achieve that goal and then follow it up with listing all the enjoyment and benefits that you will have by achieving your goals. How would you feel?

Make a Commitment – Many traders jump from one system to another and often will not fully utilize what they buy. Make a commitment that whenever you buy a product, you will use it. You need to master what you learn.

Take Action – Fear is the result of inaction – procrastination. You want to conquer fear by taking action. Action breeds confidence and courage. Wishing that you had more confidence and not taking any action will not develop more confidence. Dreaming and hope will not get you to the top, only action will get you there.

Get Knowledge – You gather knowledge, practice discipline, and grow as a person. The more you learn about the markets, your approach to trading the markets and, more importantly, yourself...the more effective you become as a trader. The more effective you become, the less fearful you are. Confidence is the lack of fear. When you are confident, you can win.

Positive Focus – At the time of executing a trade, make sure that your focus is on the profit – Success, and not the loss – Fear. If you focus on fear then the loss will manifest. You must ensure that you avoid any distractions from your goal. When you get distractions or you procrastinate, always ask yourself "Is this taking me in the direction I want to go?" "What do I need to do to achieve what I want?"

Accept a Loss – Do not expect winners all the time, accept that you will also lose often, and learn from your losing trade and move on. One of the greatest barriers to success as a trader is the fear of a loss. So long as you are disciplined and follow your system you have nothing to fear. Failure is part of the business, it is only a small battle lost, but learning from your losses will enable you to win the war. Confidence will come from NOT FEARING that you are wrong.

Patience and Persistence

In this day and age of instant gratification, people want thrills without risks, wine without alcohol, more money without effort, beer without belly and yes, a profitable trade without doing homework. Traders who lack skill expect results without effort.

The skilled master trader is fully aware of the difficulties in achieving success, and accepts that with patience and persistence success will be inevitable.

The market knows better than you and I don't rush to trade, you have to have patience and wait for the right signal – A Golden Rule No Signal – No Trade. In order to succeed in life and achieve your goals you need to utilise the power of patience.

The successful trader will never rush into a decision quickly, sure they may follow their gut instincts – but they will take plenty of time researching the reasons of the trade. The master trader realizes that patience pays! Every successful trader has a special talent for 'watching and waiting' and waits until trading behaviour has dictated when to enter the market. The prudent FOREX trader specifically applies patience to his/her advantage by:

Listening To the Market.
The market is continually donating valuable trading information, and you must get into the proper frame of mind where you are in reality taking your orders from the action of the market itself or the signals your trading system is sending you. Your judgment

will become poorer from the very time that you decide you know more about the market than the market itself and you throw patience aside and give in to fear or hope.

Sitting On the Sidelines While Waiting For a Trend to Develop.

It has often been said that looking at one's screen during the trading day is like sitting in front of a slot machine and trying to resist gambling. Successful traders in FOREX have learned that they cannot buck the major price trend of the individual currency-pair they are trading. You still don't want to let impatience cause you to trade against the trend.

While patience is important not only in waiting for the right trades, it's also important in staying with the trades that are working. You must know how to wait patiently for the optimal time to sell. Selling a winner too early is not going to allow your account balance to increase exponentially. So, this is where the 'persistence' mental factor comes in as well. You can be 'patient' until the cows come home but if you don't persistently control your impulses and don't persistently follow your exit rules, then your profits won't balance out losses over time.

"Be patient with winning trades; be enormously impatient with losing trades. Remember, it is quite possible to make large sums trading/investing if we are "right" only 30% of the time, as long as our losses are small and our profits are large."

Dennis Gartman

Successful traders depend on education to learn the critical technical analysis, trading techniques, sound money management habits, and how to control emotions. This education involves many stages, individual self-study, group lessons, classroom study, and constant practice. This takes you to a near professional level. Then, they add one more dimension, individual mentoring and coaching to rise to the absolute top and remain there over their professional career.

Do you really need a mentor or a coach? The best golfer in the world thinks so! Tiger Woods pays his coach over 1 million dollars per year! Yet he makes over 50 million dollars per year. In fact, all professional athletes have coaches to help make them better. The reason you choose to spend the money on coaching is to shorten that learning curve over which all traders have to travel, while increasing your levels of success; it is a cost of doing business. Remember if you are or want to be a professional trader you, are in a business.

Today's traders are lucky in that, they have many facilities and resources available. When I started trading 2 decades ago, there were very few resources available to a retail trader, few had heard of a trading coach or a mentor, no Internet and indeed no trading forums. Trading was lonely.

After 10 years of trading, overall I was a loser. This period included major stock market crashes, such as the 87 crash, and the 91 Gulf war. Trading was tough. My trading took to a new level when I went to the Trading Expo in USA and was introduced to a trading coach.

I sought the services of a coach; the main focus of my coach was psychology, an area that I had totally ignored all these years. My life as a trader was to change forever and I have not looked back since, trading has become so easy and I am able to pick an iron-clad trade with great ease.

As I have often said, "ignore the trend at your own peril". Today I add, "If you ignore the psychology of trading you may not succeed".

"Failure is a man who has not learnt from his blunders, if you are able to cash in on that experience you are on the path to success"

Jayendra Lakhani

The key to my success has been the persistence with which I have pursued my goals. I have suffered many setbacks in life as well as trading, but never once had I decided to give up. The lesson is never ever quit. Persistence equals success. So long as your goals inspire you, you must press on. Is your goal still correct? If not, update or abandon your goal, as there is no point in clinging to a goal that no longer inspires you.

But once you set a goal, and the goal inspires you and you are passionate about it, YOU MUST pursue your goals. Lack of persistence is one of the major causes of failures, and this weakness can be overcome by taking necessary action towards achieving your goals. It is very important that you have a very strong intensity in your desires, as weak desires bring weak results.

Persistence is a great quality of great men in our history, with persistence you are more likely to achieve success and you will stand out from the rest. 7 steps to maintain your persistence;

1. **Goals** – You need to know exactly what you want to achieve.

2. **Your reason** – Once you set the goals you must have a BIG enough reason why you want this so desperately. Your reasons needs to be compelling and backed by a "burning desire" for fulfilment.

3. **Action** – You must have a plan of action on how you will achieve the goals. Always start with small steps and gradually challenge yourself.

4. **Review** – You need to constantly review your goals to see if they are still relevant and that they still inspire you, if not change them. You must evaluate your results and this will give you the opportunity to press on with your goals.

5. **Positive Focus** – Do not let negative and discouraging influences affect you, you must always be positive and only visualize success. See yourself having already achieved the goals. Daily visualization will attract what you want in life. It will attract all the opportunities towards you.

6. **Belief** – Believing is achieving. Once you have faith in your trading plans, you will not stop easily. Never ever doubt your plans, if they are not relevant change them.

7. **Buddy or a Mentor** – Get a trading buddy or a mentor who can encourage you to follow through with your goals.

These seven steps are essential if you are to achieve success as a master trader. These are the simple steps which will control your destiny. It will enable you to join the 5% club of winners. These are simple steps that will lead you to Mastery.

There is magnificent reward if you were to follow these simple steps – The choice is yours!

"Discipline is the soul of an army. It makes small numbers formidable; procures success to the weak, and esteem to all."
George Washington

SUMMARY & ACTION POINTS

1.) Write down at least 10 Golden Rules that you will religiously follow.

2.) Brainstorm and write your mission statement.

3.) As I have often said, "ignore the trend at your own peril", today I add, "if you ignore the psychology of trading you may not succeed".

4.) "Nothing in the world can take the place of Persistence. Talent will not; nothing is more common than unsuccessful men with talent. Genius will not; unrewarded genius is almost a proverb. Education will not; the world is full of educated derelicts. Persistence and determination alone are omnipotent. The slogan 'Press On' has solved and always will solve the problems of the human race."
Calvin Coolidge – President of USA 1972

5.) The 7 simple steps to maintain persistence will change your destiny. It could truly become a defining moment in your life.

CHAPTER 13
SELF-CONFIDENCE

"When you engage in systematic, purposeful action, using and stretching your abilities to the maximum, you cannot help but feel positive and confident about yourself."
Brain Tracy

Self confidence is a birth-right and we are born with self confidence. An infant or a child has more self confidence, but as they grow this confidence begins to fade, often due to the negative conditioning of the mind.

Self confidence is an attitude that is characterized by the positive belief that you are able to achieve success in your life or attain your goals. Self confidence is a very important trait you need to have in order to succeed as a trader, however there has to be a balance. We have traders with low self confidence, that, despite having a good trading system they are unable to pull the trigger. At the other extreme, we have traders who may be over-confident which could lead to over trading and sometimes not following the rules.

So, to succeed there ought to be a balance and self-confidence needs to be founded on reality. You should have realistic trading expectations, based on the risk capital available, trading skills and ability and how much effort you are prepared to put in to reach your goal.

10 Steps To Building Self-Confidence

Building self confidence can be easily achieved, so long as you have focus and determination to take necessary actions towards achieving your goals. Consider the following powerful steps as the building blocks for achieving self confidence.

1.) Positive focus – Do not waste your powerful infinite emotional energy by worrying about a challenge, instead focus positively on the challenge and take the necessary actions on areas that you have control. Do NOT indulge in negative self talk, as this can destroy your confidence.

2.) Past Success – Remind yourself of the past success on challenges that you achieved, and you simply need to focus on how you overcome the obstacles, now you simply need to replicate it.

3.) Visualise success – Imagine you are taking a winning trade. See yourself doing the research, waiting for a setup as per your trading plan. See yourself having powerful reasons to execute the trade, pull the trigger and then manage the trade, Visualise that you are taking incremental profits, you are not snatching profits but letting the profits run. Finally see yourself closing the entire position. Look at your broker statement showing a profitable trade. How do you feel? Do this exercise on a daily basis.

4.) Role Model – Don't reinvent the wheel, the shortcut to success is to follow the ways of successful traders.

5.) Write a Journal – define what self confidence means to you. Everyday write your thoughts as they come to your mind, on areas of your success and failure, and ask quality and empowering questions on how can you build on the positives and what can you do to meet the challenges?

6.) Reframe failure – As I have often said, YOU are your biggest mentor. You should learn from your losing trades, learn from your trading journal and learn from your trading diary. When Thomas Edison failed he simply said, "I have not failed, but I have successfully eliminated 1200 combinations that did not work". Accept losses, they are part of trading and your confidence should not be shaken by the losses.

7.) Past is past – The past does not equal to future, the past is over and you can do nothing about it, you can only change the future. Focus on what you can do to change the future.

8.) Action – Once you have decided what you want to change, then it calls for a massive action towards your goals. Start by taking small steps. Do today what you can do tomorrow. Avoid procrastinating, the earlier you are able to start working on your goals the better you will be able to focus on them. If you leave it too late you will end up being stressed and bothered by the deadline. If you start early, you will also be able to come out with a good quality end result.

9.) Ask – There is always a willing person to help you. To get what you want, ask for it. If you consistently ask people what you want, you will get it. The universe is waiting there to help you.

10). Pride – Have pride in yourself. Remember, you are A WINNER!

"You are capable of achieving Forex Mastery, put all excuses aside and take massive action to achieve your dreams. Think like a winner, Act like a winner."

Jayendra Lakhani

SUMMARY & ACTION POINTS

1.) What does self confidence mean to you?

2.) Visualise a past success, how do you feel?

3.) Write a daily journal for the next 30 days focusing on daily positive achievements and how you met the daily obstacles.

CHAPTER 14
MOTIVATION

"Success is not final, failure is not fatal: it is the courage to continue that counts."

Winston Churchill

To truly become a master trader, action is required. As Shakespeare said, "Action is eloquence". You cannot have a goal without an action plan. Action is needed to succeed in any areas of your life, more so in forex trading. What action you take is dependent on your motivation.

What is Motivation?

Motivation is the burning desire or an obsession to achieve your goal. The most powerful motivation comes from our beliefs and that will drive us to action. Motivation as an emotion is so powerful that it can change your life.

Why master motivation?

Without motivation you will not achieve your goals. As the saying goes "If it is to be, it's down to me." Motivation is an internal force that will drive you to take action to achieve a specific goal. The drive will often come if you have challenging and inspiring goals. You must have a big reason why you must succeed in achieving your goals, a desire to succeed, this will prompt you to take action.

10 Rules of Motivation

1. Giant goals – It is very important for you to have inspiring and challenging goals that will create the excitement and drive to produce results. We have unlimited power within us to achieve anything, but first we must be inspired to take action. We must plant the seeds in our mind to create an intense desire to succeed.

2. Big enough reason – You must have a big enough reason why you want to achieve the goals. This reason will ensure your total commitment.

3. Have a Vision – Creating a vision can be a very motivational tool. You must ask yourself what is your desired vision? You have to create it, and live it , as if it were already true. By creating a vision, it will identify a direction and purpose, and it will promote a laser like focus, which in turn will build confidence. What better way to motivate yourself?

4. Do Not Quit – Quitters never win, Winners never quit. Ensure that you finish any projects that you undertake. Only quit the project if the goal is no longer relevant to you.

5. Networking – One of the ways to motivate yourself is to network with successful people and people who share your beliefs and desires to succeed. Trading can be a lonely business, and often working on your own you can lose focus. Joining various trading groups can often provide that push.

6. Learn to fish – Give someone a fish and you'll feed him for a day, but teach him how to fish and you will feed him for life. Trading is no different. You must learn to create your own trading system that suits your trading style, rather than be dependent on other people, e.g. signal providers.

7. Passion for trading – You must love and enjoy trading, it is this passion that creates motivation, motivation creates persistence and persistence will produce the results that you desire.

8. Develop skills – you should constantly challenge yourself and develop and improve your trading skills. Never rest on past laurels, always aim to get better. Knowledge creates the motivation to take action.

9. Relax – A relaxed mind will think well. For some traders who like to work non-stop, doing nothing can actually be pretty difficult. You should always set aside some free time to do nothing. This can actually be healthy for your mind, body and emotional life, especially if you find that you're really wearing yourself down. Feel your sense of belonging to silence. This is the kind of meditation to empty your mind.

10. Accept failure – Learn from your mistakes. You will not succeed if you do not try. Keep trying and analyse what made you fail.

"When you know what you want, and you want it badly enough, you'll find a way to get it. My suggestion would be to walk away from the 90% who don't and join the 10% who do."

Jim Rohn

SUMMARY & ACTION POINTS

1.) When you achieve success, celebrate and reward yourself.

2.) Set a good example by being a positive role model.

CHAPTER 15
SELF-SABOTAGE

"Self-sabotage is when we say we want something and then go about making sure it doesn't happen."

Alyce P Cornby (American author)

What is self-sabotage behaviour?

Self-sabotage behaviour is when there is no logical or rational explanation for why you can't do the things you want to do or why you can't have the things you want to have. As a trader you would often take decisions that are against your best interest as a result losing the opportunity to succeed.

You are suffering from self sabotage, if you

- Procrastinate

- Never achieve goals

- You worry too much

- You are struggling all the time

- You have unfulfilled dreams

- You experience self doubt

- Inability to control anger

How do I break free from my self-sabotage behaviour?

Self Esteem – Focus on your strengths and how you can build on them. Look at areas that you can easily do NOW, this will boost your confidence. Body language – act confidently, visualise success.

Take responsibility – Master trader realizes that there is no one to blame, and the individual trader must accept all the credit for success or the responsibility if the trade goes against him. Master trader believes that only he can influence his trading success.

Trade the plan – Follow your golden rule of - No Signal No Trade!

Take breaks – Stay away from the screen. Do not sit in front of the screen watching for trades all the time. Take breaks on a regular basis. You can always use the technology to give you alerts when a certain price level is reached. Watching the screen all the time could result in you taking a trade when there was no signal.

Mental checklist – I believe that you must have at least 3 good reasons for a low risk high probability trade. Ensure that you have confluence of indicators

Mental rehearsals – Place yourself in a calm and relaxed state of mind, mentally rehearse following your trading plan when executing a trade, once the trade is taken mentally visualise that you are managing the trade. The sole object is to minimize the loss and maximize your gain.

Self Confidence – Self-confidence is a measure of your belief in yourself and your trading system. It follows that you trust and follow your trading plan. If you lack self-confidence then it is likely that you will not follow your best trading plan, or even a winning trade signal. To gain the confidence of your trading plan you must do extensive back testing, follow it up with demo trading and then finally start live trading with real money on a mini account and gradually increasing the trade size when you have successful trades. You must earn the right to increase the trade size.

Affirmations – Develop a positive mindset by focusing on success. By using powerful positive thinking techniques, creative visualizations and positive affirmations, it is possible to achieve whatever you want. Affirmations are short positive statements which target a subconscious mind with positive beliefs. These positive statements enable us to focus on our goals.

Let go of the past – Are you a captive of your past failures? If not you need to let go and liberate yourself from this behaviour. Instead use this energy to think about the life that you can create today.

Get rid of toxic people – Toxic people will pull you down; their negative energy will affect your thoughts and actions. Limit your interaction with them, if they do nothing to transform your life.

Develop connections – Develop connections with sources of positive emotional energy. Look for people who can support you and help you to fulfil your ambitions. Look for a mentor, a trading buddy – any person who will motivate you and give you the push when you need it.

"All of us have infinite potential but most of us are self-sabotaging."

SUMMARY & ACTION POINTS

1.) Identify any tendency that you may have to sabotage yourself. Write down your thoughts and ask questions, what do you need to do to fight this menace?

2.) **Visualise success** – You get what you focus on, so expect nothing but success. Feel the pleasure of achieving success.

3.) Just think where you could take yourself if you could put as much energy and creativity into manifesting your goals, as you do procrastinating and avoiding them!

CHAPTER 16
OVERCOMING TRADING FEAR

"No matter how hard you try to succeed as a trader, If your focus is on the fear of a losing trade, your fear will manifest. Fear of a loss attracts a loss"

Jayendra Lakhani

How do you define fear "a strong emotion caused by anticipation or awareness of danger, it implies anxiety and usually the loss of courage." This definition of fear is useful in helping define the issues that traders face when coping with fear. The reality is that all traders feel fear at some level, but the key is how we prepare to address our concerns related to taking on risk as a trader.

Mark Douglas, in his book, Trading in the Zone, says that most investors believe they know what is going to happen next. This causes traders to put too much weight on the outcome of the current trade, while not assessing their performance as "a probability game" that they are playing over time. This manifests itself in investors getting too high and too low and causes them to react emotionally, with excessive fear or greed after a series of losses or wins.

Your trading success is dependent on your belief in your trading system. The greatest reason traders fail is fear, and fear can arise from your lack of belief in your trading system. All traders will encounter fear at some stage, no matter whether you are a professional or a novice trader, this seems inevitable, and to succeed and fight fear, traders will have to work through this positively. Winning traders manage their fear, while losers are controlled by it. Winners take positive action in spite of their fears.

Wisdom is the correct use of your skills as a trader and those skills are gained by experience. Experience will come from taking ACTION and following your trading system. Fear may immobilize your decision making process resulting into incorrect analysis or even leading to procrastination.

Two of the greatest fears that a trader will encounter, can be;

1. Fear of loss.

2. Fear of letting a profit turn into a loss.

Fear of a Loss

No matter how skilled you may be in your technical analysis, your fundamental analysis, or your having devised some brilliant trading strategies – you may still face roadblocks of becoming a successful and a profitable Trader. Why? – Overcoming fear of losing money. I have never met a trader who really likes losing money – at the same time I have never come across any Trader who has NEVER lost any money. A leading "guru" on charts and technical analysis in UK, who regularly lectures at seminars, once admitted that despite being brilliant in his study of technical analysis, he has failed miserably in his trading, having blown his account many times – now he just concentrates on teaching trading to others!

Fear of losing is not a problem, but it is how you handle the loss. A trader, who is relaxed, can look forward to another trade. Your success or failure in trading depends on your attitude towards your gains as well as losses – and how you handle them.

The market does not know that you exist. You, or for that matter, any trader cannot do anything to change the market or influence it. Only YOU can control your behaviour. Whether it is a big drawdown on an account, or a good profitable trade, a professional trader uses his head to stay calm and will look for his new trade. Only a novice trader will become excited and depressed. You are simply wasting your precious nervous energy!

The primary difference between a professional trader and a novice is how they handle a loss. One of the greatest reasons for a lack of success in trading is that most traders play it safe, they are so afraid of losing that they simply do not pull the trigger, even when they have a great trade! To a professional trader, winning means being unafraid to lose.

Imagine how many times you fell down before you finally learnt to ride a bike? Or how many times the baby fell down before the child went from crawling to walking to running?

So for most novice traders, the reason they do not win in their trading is because the pain of losing money is far greater than the joy of being a winning trader. On the other hand losing inspires a professional trader, for he will look at that as a way to learn from that loss and he will always ask the question, how can I profit the next time. The winning trader will have a trading journal, where he records his trade; he will pull out the chart, and study it carefully to see why the trade made a loss. A professional trader is more concerned about avoiding a big loss and less concerned about small losses.

What is important is how well you execute your trading plan and stay focused with ruthless discipline. With a good Trading Plan you should have entry and exit strategies, which you can act upon decisively and without hesitation.

Fear of letting a profit turn into a loss

I am often asked when I take my profit. - I simply say "Go with the trend! – let the profits run, and cut the losses short" But what do most Traders do? They SNATCH PROFITS and let the losses run! Too many traders want to lock in a quick profit to guarantee they feel like a winner.

So when do you take profits? For example I tend to break my trade into 2 or 4 lots, depending on what time frame I am trading.

So let's say If I am trading a shorter term time frame, I break my trade in 2 lots, so that as soon as I am say 30 points in profit, I close 50% of my trade and than for the remaining I move my stop to break even. This way I am guaranteed that I will not lose! I will let the second lot run and I am seeking to ride the position with a trailing stop on the remaining portion of the position. Letting your winners run ensures a healthy increase in your equity balance – imagine if you catch a "big move" in 2 out 5 trades – what would that do to your confidence? The key is patience.

If however, I were trading a longer term time frame, I would break the trade in 4 or more parts, taking 25% profits gradually, and at the same time trying to catch the big move. This strategy has given me the most confidence.

So just how do you achieve faith in your system, the discipline and patience? In my opinion, for a novice trader, it is vitally important to have some sort of consultancy from experienced traders or have a trader's coach to guide them. The amount you spend on being mentored; will more than be paid for not only from the profits that you will make as a result – but also from the losses that you will not sustain. Refer to the section "a trading coach" for more information.

You have a choice, and only YOU, can make that decision.

How do I break free from FEAR?

Belief – If you knew that you could handle anything that came your way and that you had a great trading system, which WILL deliver CONSISTENT profits. What would you possibly have to fear? – Nothing, there will be no fear at all. To remove this fear, all you have to do is to have belief in your trading system, and follow it consistently each time it produces a signal.

Action – Fears only enemy is action. Action can remove fear in an instant, but it has to be the right type of action. The ability to take ACTION reduces the paralysis of fear and will build your self-confidence. Fear can lead to procrastination but if you correctly do your homework and follow your Golden Rule of No Signal – No Trade, then this should lead to confidence, a winning trader acts rationally by following his trading plan. On the other hand you could also see a trader take action but irrationally. His actions will be guided by greed and the thought of outsmarting the market. The market is always right, no matter how crazy it becomes, you cannot fight it or control it, but to succeed you just flow with it and follow it.

Focus – You must focus and concentrate on the immediate action that is required of you to move forward, i.e. the trade that you intend to take. Do not have anything else in mind apart from the focus, the analysis and signal which is being generated by your system. Analyse it fully and look for at least 3 reasons why you must take this trade. Narrowing focus on just that one area, removes distractions and you are able to analyze the trade better.

Money management – Any system will not be 100%, so long as you keep your losses to a minimum and let your winners run, you are likely to make substantial profits over a longer term. So the key is cut your losses and manage your trades.

Master of one – do not try and be jack of all trades, instead concentrate on just one or two strategies, get to know the behaviour of these setups well. For example I have many members who only trade a divergence setup and nothing else. The system has been automated to look for divergence, and when this occurs, they trade. Focusing on just a few areas can remove the stress from trading and therefore help with better focus and so removes the fear in some ways.

Get the edge – Trading is no rocket science, in fact it is a child's play. Focus on the KISS principle and look for a low risk high probability trade, and have the necessary discipline to never deviate from your system.

Scared money – Never ever use scared money for trading, as this often causes the fear of losing money. Often you will be so anxious to succeed that you will snatch the profits, to feel good about a winning trade. Also some traders will panic at the first sign of a small loss and bail out, only to see the market moving substantially in their favour, without them on board. Do your homework, and follow your rules, then give the trade a chance to work for you or against you. Patience is the key.

"Too many traders focus on avoiding a loss instead of focusing on the opportunity, as a consequence they miss out on the profitable opportunity."

Jayendra Lakhani

SUMMARY & ACTION POINTS

1.) The only way to fight fear is to take action.

2.) Use your trading journal as a learning experience. Experience and confidence fights fear head on.

3.) Your thoughts are created by YOU – you are in control of what goes in your mind.

4.) Positive thinking needs daily practice. Write down your affirmations, and visualise on these positive statements everyday – ideally 3 times a day.

5.) Before a trade is taken, following your trading plan, focus on a win trade.

CHAPTER 17
DISCIPLINE

"We must all suffer from one of two pains: the pain of discipline or the pain of regret. The difference is discipline weighs ounces while regret weighs tons."

Jim Rohn

A master trader succeeds because he is disciplined to follow his trading plan, and follow the Golden Rule of No Signal – No Trade.

In my opinion a successful trader needs three things;

1. Trading System – a system, which will allow the trader to pull the trigger, from which he can profit.

2. Money Management techniques – Having pulled the trigger, you need to place the stop to limit the risk of any loss. It is also important that the stop loss is not moved further when the price gets nearer the stop, and

3. The most important of all- Discipline, Discipline and Discipline! – Trade the signals as per your trading plan. As always your Golden Rule must be No Signal – No Trade!

So what is Discipline? One of the reasons why many traders are unable to be disciplined is because they have not defined it.

Discipline – form a habit of regular and systematic action; to bring under control so as to act systematically. "The habit of obedience."

Trading Discipline – To pull the trigger when your trading system gives you the signal, followed by sound money management rules. You have a set of rules that you will follow, and will only act, if your system says so.

The key word in the above definition is "habit" – so discipline in trading is the practice of forming a habit of following your trading plan. Discipline will involve the need to act consistently, in a reliable manner, and in accordance with your trading strategy, which you set forth in your trading plan.

It is said that 90% of traders lose money, and more shocking statistics is 10% of traders go bankrupt, so why would this be the case if say most of the traders were aware of discipline or were exercising discipline? All individual traders have their own needs and it will vary from person to person, for example a certain task to one person may require tremendous amount of self control and discipline, whereas the same task to another person may not require any effort.

To practice discipline in trading, two things are most important, these are;

Trading System – You have to regularly monitor your trading systems with the changes in the market and also your style of trading. If there were changes in the products that you trade, i.e. for example if you were trading stocks, then the system you may have used will not be relevant for the forex market, because the behaviour, patterns, volume etc are totally different in a Forex market, so your trading system should reflect what products you are trading. In order to devise a trading system, you have to make plans and have patience, to go through all areas of trading. Having designed a system you must ensure that you implement it – Many traders fail to implement the system, mostly due to fear. Fear of profit or fear of loss, fear is also the most important aspect in the psychology of trading and I have a full chapter on this topic.

Money Management - Must have discipline to follow sound money management. For example a trader has 70% of winning trades, but if the overall loss from 30% of trades exceeds the total profit then he is a loser. The bottom line is how much you take home! Small losses should not turn into large losses, and equally important you should not snatch your profits. Once again here if you implement your trading system, than large losses can be contained – ability to do this is discipline!

As part of my trading system, as soon as I pull the trigger to open a new position, I immediately put a stop loss. Once the position is in profit, often I will start closing some of the positions gradually. Depending on the market conditions, I would close at least 25% of my position for a profit of 20 to 50 pips, than another 25% for 75 pips+; thereafter I would be using trailing stops for the rest of the position, using the moving averages and other indicators to keep me in the trade. Using this method I have been able to pocket several hundred pips from the final trade! As I keep saying Currencies trend very well – so ride the trend.

One forex trader I am mentoring "never" closes any of his positions – he always gets stopped out. He has 70% of his trades being stopped out between breakeven to 50 pips maximum. He starts with a 50 pip stop loss than will gradually have a trailing stop. His 70% of losing trades has averaged a loss of 25 pips per trade, so for 7 trades that would be 175 pips. However the 30% of winning trades he has averaged a profit of 179 pips per trade, so for 3 trades that is a profit of 537 pips. Therefore that would be a net gain of 362 pips for 10 trades, yet 70% of trades were losing. This is working smartly, being disciplined to cut losses and letting the profits run.

I discuss some of these strategies in my video tutorials, once again the bottom line is not how many losing trades you have, but how much you take home!

How can you improve your discipline?
Your trading should be treated as a business, nothing less; it should not be a hobby. Any business organisation will have goals, they will have Budgets prepared in which they will detail the sources of its revenues and against it there will be a budget of its outgoings – the net of this are profits. The company will measure its performance against the budget and will attempt to take action on any variances, and will look at reasons why the performance is positive or negative.

Your trading should not be any different. In the case of your Trading you have to compare your actual performance with your system, e.g. is your performance better than the system? The losing or winning trades you had, do they mirror the system? If not why is it different? Why did you not follow the System? Did you have a loss, which should not have occurred if you followed your system?

I am regularly comparing my performance with my trading system, so how have I coped with this? Well for a start, I don't trade that often, and when I do I need an "iron clad" signal – I have patience to wait. I keep a trading journal, which will record full details of my trade together with a copy of the chart, on which I will write notes. I have a full page trade journal, and on each page I have various inspiration quotes to motivate myself. My trading journal will have the following information;

- The chart with all my trend lines and indicators.

- Reasons for placing the trade, at least 3 reasons.

- Entry date & Time, Price, stop, and initial target.

- Exit date & time, price.

- Profit/Loss.

- Comments & lessons learned.

You can download this form from my website. **www.4x4u.net**

In the comments section, I will examine the position in detail, and determine the reasons of the loss. Until you know the cause, you will not be able to change it. Without having a trading discipline, you are doomed to fail; it is no good having a great system if you do not have the discipline to follow it. Trading discipline should be your number one priority.

Tips to give you More Discipline

To succeed in trading you must condition your mind to follow the rules of discipline over and over again. I always recommend my members to read their Golden Rules every day, before they start trading. As you read out you must visualise taking these actions. Those members who start the day with these simple trading prayers often tend to be successful as they are constantly reminding themselves to follow their rules.

You may want to review the following major rules of discipline which you must incorporate as part of your trading;

Take responsibility for your actions
Only YOU determine what to do and how to do it, so if anything goes wrong you take responsibility and cannot look to blame anyone else. You have to set yourself free by taking control over the rest of your life.

Mistakes
You have to analyse your mistakes, the mistakes you make are in some way related to the negative mental states – whether it is an inability to pull the trigger or compulsiveness, you can trace it to a negative mental state.

Discipline = Profit
You have a choice, either you are disciplined and let the market pay you a handsome return, or you can be undisciplined and continue to lose. The choice is yours!

Discipline involves controlling your mental state.

"Delusions are states of mind which, when they arise within our mental continuum, leave us disturbed, confused and unhappy. Therefore, those states of mind which delude or afflict us are called 'delusions' or 'afflictive emotions'."
His Holiness the Dalai Lama

In my opinion the most destructive negative mental attitude or delusional emotion is anger. Anger is an emotion that destroys more people, relationships and businesses than all the illness in the world. People seem so angry all the time. Imagine what this does to your trading results. Smile and the world smiles back at you, learn to be a happy person, this will do wonders for your bottom line.

It must be emphasized that to completely eliminate negative emotions from your mind is a lengthy psychological process, requiring study, mindfulness, reflection and honest observation of one's mind.

To begin with, meditation is an ideal way to try and conquer the negative mental attitudes, it will not only give you insight into what anger is and what happens to oneself when feeling angry, but it also has a calming effect, tends to relax your mind and body. I always start my day with prayers and meditation.
If you are unable to control your mental state, than you simply cannot trade profitably. In my opinion if this applies to you, then you must consider giving up trading until such time as you are able to control your mental state. You should seek professional guidance in this matter, and certainly there are a few good quality trader coaches who specialise in such areas.

PASSION

This gives you the driving force to enjoy the process. Most successful traders have true love or passion about their trading. Ok they are in it for the money, which is the end result, but they enjoy reading the charts, designing the trading system, pulling the trigger. What is the point of being disciplined if you do not enjoy the process.

"A man is only truly great, when he acts from passion." Passion is defined as having great deal of emotion or feeling. So how we get passion? The same way we get love and warmth, we have to decide on it and feel it. In the same way, you also have to have love for trading. For example my son says to me, I don't care how much money I make trading, what is important is how can I become greater than Warren Buffet? To him that is his driving force, his goal – by having this passion built into your psychology, the target gets nearer.

EARN THE RIGHT TO TRADE BIG

If you can trade 1 lot profitably what makes you think that you can trade 10 lots successfully. I always advise traders to start with a mini account and after each successful week you increase the trade sizes. Taking small steps, achieving them and then challenging yourself by increasing the bet sizes. What you should not do is trade a big size after a losing trade because you are trying to recover a loss from a previous trade. In fact you should do the opposite.

CUT THE LOSERS AND LET THE WINNERS RUN

You are a loser if you do not get out of a losing trade. Many traders tend to let the losers run and cut the profits. Whereas it should be the other way round. You should cut the losers and let the profits run. For example you can still be a winner with only 30% of your trades being profitable, if you were to follow a simple rule of cut the losses and let the winners run!

MARKETS ARE THERE EVERYDAY

Never put yourself in a position of wanting the excitement of trading each session, or every hour, only your brokers will benefit from this. If you miss a trade opportunity, do not focus on the missed opportunity but focus on the new opportunities that exist now and in future. Markets are there all the time. Never cry over missed trades and never chase the markets, give the markets time to settle down and wait for a confirmation of a signal.

DONT HOPE AND PRAY

If you have a losing trade and the signal has reversed, get out and even consider reversing the position. Take a small loss and move on! Hope and prayers do not work. God has better things to do and will not intervene. You just need to get out and cut your losses!

SPECULATE AND YOU LOSE

There is no room for speculation and gambling, for that you can play the lottery or go to a casino. Ruthlessly follow your Golden Rule: No Signal – No Trade! Don't be a speculator, you want to be a master trader.

TRADING JOURNAL

As I have often said, you are your biggest mentor. Your trading journal has a wealth of information that no guru or a mentor will give. Love your losers, learn from them and ensure that the mistakes are not repeated!

PATIENCE

All good trades will come to those traders who wait for a setup. Patience is waiting for a setup to occur and once the setup occurs you POUNCE hard, at this stage you cannot afford to procrastinate. In the meantime, whilst you are waiting for a setup, you should do something else. Read a book, do your stretches, breathing exercises, meditation or just simply relax. Do anything but do not sit in front of your screen for hours waiting for a setup to occur.

Once in a trade, be patient and give the trade time to either work for you or work against you. If it is not giving you a quick profit than have patience and stay in the trade as long as the signal is in your favour. Only close the trade if the signal reverses and the trade does not do what you expect it to do.

TAKE INCREMENTAL PROFITS

I strongly advocate breaking your positions into multi lots, say 2 portions, and as the market is moving in your favour you want to scale out of your winners. Take profit for the first lot, and review the stop for the remaining position. You can have a trailing stop loss, i.e. you can follow dynamic support/resistance levels, for example the 13 or 55 ema. After taking incremental profit and reviewing your stops, you now have a free trade and that is a fantastic position to be in.

REPETITION IS THE MOTHER OF ALL SKILLS

Become an expert in your methodology, execute it to perfection, and keep repeating the success day by day, week by week and year by year. Only review your trading plan if it stops doing what you want. Repetition gives you the skill, and puts you on the road to mastery.

PARALYSIS BY ANALYSIS

Over analysis leads to confusion resulting in procrastination, to succeed follow the KISS principle. Only have a few indicators and important information on the charts. Majority of my charts only have Price, moving averages, and MACD. Just these simple indicators can give me a consistent 1000 pips per month.

RESPECT THE MARKET

Finally........ RESPECT the market. The market may be crazy if it is going too high, for example like it did during the NASDAQ boom. Just flow with the markets, do not fight it, and do not try and be smart thinking that you are more clever than the market. Don't try and pick the tops or bottoms. Let the market do what it wants – just follow it.

Be disciplined in following the simple rules above, condition your mind and you will be rewarded.

RULES TO AVOID

Unfortunately, amateur traders are often led to believe and follow the wrong set of rules, and often you will have so many conflicting rules given by various market "gurus". This conflict often leads to sabotage by the trader due to confusion.

Here are some of the rules that are widely practiced by amateur traders, often picked up from "free seminars".

NEVER TURN A WINNER INTO A LOSER

This rule says never be greedy and take a small profit. Opportunities exist in the market all the time and you will make many trades throughout the day and many more tomorrow.

Jayendra Says: Always adhere to sound money management principles, but do not snatch profits. Why take 20 pips profit when there are 100 pips on the table? It is a crime. The Bindal FX system has a strategy how you can run your winners and cut your losses. Can you imagine the stress caused by multiple trades during the day? What would be better? One trade with a profit of 60 pips, or ten trades with a profit of 30 pips? Over-trading can lead to losing trades, not to mention the mental stress.

Become an Expert.

Many Gurus advocate complete understanding of technical analysis and fundamental analysis, to ensure market success. Become an expert in technical and fundamental analysis.

Jayendra Says: I choose to differ. We are now inundated with so much technical analysis, advanced charting packages, proprietary software, new indicators, and never ending commentaries from "gurus", many of them don't even trade! All this analysis leads to paralysis leading to confusion and a wrong action as a result. One of my graduate members consistently banks over 600 pips per month using just the chart and moving averages – No MACD, No RSI, and NO Stochastic! – So how does he do it? Following the KISS principle.

My advice would be to devise a simple strategy using one methodology from the Bindal FX system, learn it fully, become a master of it and follow it with discipline. Do not change methodologies from day to day. Master one strategy at a time before you learn more. There is no place for traders who are jack of all trades, often they are the biggest losers.

Every time an amateur trader goes to a seminar, learns a new strategy and starts applying it, only to discard it when another "Guru" shows him another strategy. Many traders jump from one strategy to another, one day they are trading divergence, next day they think only a pivot system will deliver the results. Losers also do not have the patience to stick with a basket of currencies to trade; they hop from one currency to another. One day they focus on GBP, next day they move to oil because a "guru" says oil prices are exploding. Then they decide to look at GBPJPY because it is very volatile and he thinks he can become rich instantly. GBPJPY is abandoned and now he focuses on Gold because he receives an email from a trading guru stating that gold is about to hit $1000! The search continues......

Become an expert in one or a few currency pairs. Every currency or stock will have a different behaviour pattern. Focus and learn about it, understand the pattern inside out, only then move on to another currency pair. A few of my graduate members only focus on GBPJPY; they have over 70% winners with an average pip profit of over 150 pips per trade, whereas the losing trades averages less than 50 pips. What they have done is become "expert" on one rather than expert on none!

FUNDAMENTAL NEWS

I have often said that the chart knows the news! Too many amateur traders focus on fundamental news as they are being released and spend countless hours listening to their "gurus" on Bloomberg or CNBC all day long. Many of these so called gurus have no clue about the markets and I wonder if they indeed trade them!

Fundamental reporting is all news and history. The story has already been acted upon by the professional market participants. Do not trade the reports. It is too late. It is better to miss that market move immediately after news, wait for the markets to settle down and then move in on a good 123 retracement pattern. Often this news creates a false breakout, divergence patterns and the price will often move exactly up to a support/resistance line, a dynamic EMA, Pivots or Fibonacci. Use the price volatility during the news release to your advantage – don't get sucked into a trade.

"Discipline is the soul of an army. It makes small numbers formidable; procures success to the weak, and esteem to all."
George Washington

SUMMARY & ACTION POINTS

1.) Draw up a list of 10 Golden Rules that you will follow.

2.) Why must you follow each of these Golden rules?

3.) What are the consequences of NOT following the golden rules?

CHAPTER 18

A TRADING COACH

"Smart people learn from experience. Super smart people learn from other people's experience."

John Bytheway

The naked truth is that the market preys on your fear and ignorance around trading. Most people are more comfortable talking about their sex life than their trading success or failures.
In fact, many people are downright embarrassed that they don't know all about investing in stocks. It's time to come out of the dark ages and realize that these are learned skills like any other skill that you've already mastered and that all you need is the right coach.

- Top athletes like Tiger Woods and Andre Agassi use performance coaches to stay at the top of their game.
- Oscar winning actors use acting coaches.
- Award winning singers use voice coaches.
- Successful Traders use a trading coach.

If you want to become financially free you must reject conventional ways of thinking and follow proven methods that work. The real key to wealth is your thinking process.
A trading coach is a trusted counsellor, guide, or a tutor. There is no reason to stumble and fall when you have someone guiding you around the blocks in the road.

I consider trading skills to be one of the most difficult to acquire, yet very few traders take on a coach or a mentor to help them. All professionals, in every field get the best coaches these days, yet traders fail to do this. A trader's coach helps you to develop the ability to achieve higher levels of success in all areas of your life. Every part of a trader's life will affect his performance.

The ability for a trader to follow his trading system for entering and exiting a trade is what traders call "the discipline of trading." Without having discipline you will never have the consistency necessary to improve your technical skills. If you do not have a good foundation of technique, you will not master the art of trading. What good is the best system in the world if you cannot follow it? This is one of the reasons why traders need coaching.

Another reason a traders coach is valuable to a trader is when a trader wants to break out of a comfortable level of good performance and move to the next level to be a trading master. Just like top athletes have coaches to observe and give feed back to increase performance, so too can a trader benefit from top performance coaching as well

Do you want to become a better trader without losing your entire trading account in the process? Trading coaches are not cheap, but in my opinion they are a lot cheaper than the losses which many traders make in the markets. It is not difficult to make money from the markets, but first you have to learn the mechanics of how you go about doing it.

How can you benefit from a Trading Coach?

A trading coach often is familiar with the trading environment and has years of experience from which to draw. They are someone whose work or accomplishments you admire and would like to model in your own career. The mentor relationship is one that is built on respect and is exclusively focused on your professional development and success. He or she can offer unbiased advice and share wisdom that will allow you to grow and reach your full potential.

Your mentor can also help you to avoid mistakes many young professionals make, steer clear of common pitfalls and serve as an unbiased beacon with your best interest at heart. Additionally, a relationship with a mentor helps you to utilize two of the quickest methods for personal development: modelling and emulation. The success principles that work for one person will usually work for another. Therefore, as you model and emulate the desired behaviour(s) of your mentor, you will quickly improve your skill set, expand your professional and business knowledge and jump-start your results.

What can a coach do for you?

A coach, on the other hand, is a professional whose work is focused on helping you manifest your inner self -- your needs, passion and desire to contribute -- to achieve success. The coach's guidance is more personal and specific and the results are often quick and dramatic.

"The decision to work with a coach is intimate, personal and totally confidential," said Anneli Driessen, author of "Ultimate Success: Seven Secrets to Spiritually-Based Leadership."
"It is based upon the integrity of both people involved. If the client is willing to be absolutely open, honest and to offer complete disclosure, the results can be staggering," Driessen said.

There are many trading coaches today who can offer you quality guidance. I myself do some coaching, but as my main focus is trading the markets I only do a limited amount of coaching each year. I would have no hesitation in recommending the services of other successful trading coaches. I myself have used the services of Adrienne Toghraie, of Trading on Target.

As I mentioned earlier, this course changed my life as a trader. I was impressed with Adrienne's The Winning Edge books. The course is realistically priced and Adrienne has tapes aimed at specific trading problems, e.g. discipline, motivation, self-confidence, and a trading plan.

Coaching is a powerful partnership that can save you time and money by helping you avoid dangerous pitfalls and dead end paths whilst accelerating your financial journey. Your coach will provide support and accountability for your goals while mentoring you with valuable insights. Your personal coach will help you see perspectives you didn't even know existed, and will help you overcome the inevitable bumps and hurdles that develop along your journey to financial freedom.

Your personal coach isn't biased by commissions or advertising dollars. Your coach is paid for one thing – to help you reach your goals and live the life you dreamed about. Most importantly, you will improve your trading performance. The difference between your current level of success and the level you desire to reach is largely – perhaps almost entirely – psychological. These mental barriers can be subtle, small, and insidious. But their impact can be extreme. A trading coach will isolate your deficiencies and then help you find ways to help you break through to a much higher level of profitability.

Why do you need a coach? Ask Tiger Woods.

"Live as if you were to die tomorrow. Learn as if you were to live forever."

Mahatma Gandhi

SUMMARY & ACTION POINTS

1.) Do you need a Mentor? If so list all areas of your trading as well as trading psychology that need attention.

2.) What are you expecting the mentor to do for you?

3.) Take time to find your mentors. Ask around, recommended mentors are the best. Do not be afraid to interview your mentor, as it is YOU who is hiring their services.

CHAPTER 19
THE SECRETS OF
MASTER TRADERS

"What comes out of you when you are squeezed is what is inside you".

Wayne Dyer

One of the most important things that affect trading has to be self-discipline. Self-discipline is simply a mental technique to stay focussed on the trading skills that you need to acquire, to take actions to implement your trading system, and to accomplish your goals.

Stay focused on what you need to learn.
You need to focus on education, on how you can improve and implement your trading plan, rather than focus on the money. If you are successful trader than you will have the money, which is the by product of your success. Every professional, these days has to have continuous professional development, so that they keep pace with the new market environment, so why should traders be any different? You should always keep learning and improving.

Take Complete Responsibility
You and only you alone are completely responsible for whatever you end up with. You will never meet a successful trader who is looking to blame someone or something else for his or her losses.

This is a critical step in understanding how to become a successful trader because until you take complete responsibility for all of your trades, you will never feel comfortable with your system and you will never reap the rewards. Additionally, when something goes wrong with a trade, the traders who take complete responsibility for their actions will look at those "failures" as learning experiences. The trader who takes responsibility will try and determine what went wrong and what needs to be done in order to avoid similar mistakes in the future. The trader who does not take complete responsibility will simply say "the market wasn't right" or "my broker is an idiot". That trader will likely make the same mistakes again and will never understand why he/she cannot win in the stock market. This step is critical. Before all else, you must accept everything that you do as your responsibility.

Dealing With Losses
You should strictly follow your money management rules, otherwise you are doomed to fail. When you enter the trade you should confront with the possibility that you could be wrong, and if you are wrong, what will be the amount you will lose and what impact it will have on your trading capital. Therefore when confronting losses, you are not trading from the position of fear and as a result the possibility of a losing trade will not create any pain. You will simply accept the loss and move onto the next trade.

Become an Expert with One Market Behaviour
Lots of traders tend to confuse themselves with too many conflicting indicators and tend to over analyse the trend, this leads to confusion – paralysis by analysis. To become an expert, choose one simple trading system that identifies a pattern on a chart. You want to understand every aspect of this pattern and it's behaviour, you are going to focus just on that pattern for the time being. This may mean that you may let go of other opportunities that arise, but what you will be doing is building a base of confidence from concentrating in a small area and you will be able to trade with more confidence. Obviously once you think that you are trading successfully with this pattern, than you can try and move on and learn other patterns.

One of my students, virtually makes a living out of trading MACD divergence on all currencies, and has a great success rate, which even a professional trader will envy! And to add to the divergence he will add a few candle chart patterns. Presently he is earning several hundred pips each month just trading divergence. He has become an expert in this, and within minutes will know if he sees an "iron clad" pattern.

He intends to learn other areas of market behaviours, such as pivot point trading and moving average crossovers at a later stage.

Plan the Trade and Trade the Plan.

The point of this rule is that once you have developed a system that is right for you, then you must stick to it no matter what. As a result, your plan must be able to cater for every eventuality. Once you put your money down then you no longer control what happens. You won't know what the prices will do so you can't worry about anything except following your plan. What will your entry be? What will your exit be? What happens if the price gets close to your stop order? Do you see what I'm getting at? You don't want to have to answer these questions AFTER you put your money down! You want everything to be automatic by that point. So make sure that your system plans for everything.

Execute your Trading System Confidently

The proper execution of your trades is one of the most important aspects of becoming a successful trader, which is an art that most traders find so difficult to learn.

Many successful traders have discovered and developed a system that fits them best. Once you have spent lot of time developing the system and rules you should stick with it and don't try and out guess the system, as it will lead to extreme frustration and possibly losses in the long term.

Most good trading system will make consistent money from the markets over the long term, you must have faith in your system and try and follow it if it is successful. If you are not comfortable with your system than you will always be tempted to break it.

Positive Self-Belief

Successful traders know that it is the discipline displayed in following their rules that makes all the difference. If you do not believe in yourself and your system then you are going to have difficulty following your rules. Following your rules is the most important aspect of successful trading. But even if you do follow all your rules, if you are constantly doubting yourself then you aren't going to have any fun at all, plain and simple. On the other hand If you do not have belief in yourself then there may be a problem with your system... it may not be suited for you.

Keep Trading as part of a Balanced Life.
Have fun and have a life outside of Trading. Trading is stressful, so do everything you can think of to eliminate this stress. I have met many successful traders and one thing they all have in common is their lack of stress. They all have hobbies, families, friends, sports, and leisure activities that allow them to follow their rules without stressing about every move. It's amazing!

Monitor your performance
You should be disciplined enough to have an audit of all your actions, have a trading journal for all trades with reasons on why you entered the trade. All trades once closed must be analysed to see all successes and failures. Focus on the failures and see what could have been done to improve upon them.

Just like any business, you should main a set of accounts. You should have a profit & loss account with a balance sheet, for your trading activities. Your profits should be after you have paid yourself. Only then can you have a true picture of your success.

Learn from your mistakes
Find out what works for you. Use your trading journal and learn from this. Repeat over and over again what works for you, and learn from what you did wrong in previous trades. Take every trade as a lesson and use it to improve the way you trade.

Knowledge is Power
You must always strive to learn better and powerful ways to make money from the markets, learn ways to personal development. As soon as you have achieved mastery in one methodology, try to learn other methods that can enhance the way you trade. For

example you can look at options trading as a way to hedge your portfolio.

"Risk comes from not knowing what you're doing."
Warren Buffet

SUMMARY & ACTION POINTS

1.) In your opinion, who are the greatest Investors of all time and why?

2.) In your opinion, who are the greatest traders of all time and why?

3.) List the 10 qualities that they have. Would you want those qualities?

4.) List the top 5 biographies that you have read.

5.) List the top 5 books that you have read, in just one paragraph what were the major learning points from these books?

6.) List 5 books that you intend to read within the next 12 months.

"Everyone has brainpower to follow the stock market. If you made it through fifth-grade math, you can do it."
Peter Lynch

CHAPTER 20
FOREX TRADING TIPS

"The opportunity of the lifetime must be seized during the lifetime of the opportunity."

Leonard Ravenhill

Money Management Rules

Please remember to exercise good equity management in all your trades. There are no hard rules on this, you should do what suits your trading style rather than do what I tell you or what the so called "Forex Guru" says. Whilst most books talk about 2% of your margin account on a single trade, or 20 pips. I personally tend to have an open mind, and my stops will be based on the trading opportunity which is presented to me, often I could have a trade with just 10 pips stop and sometimes when I am using say a weekly chart, I may even have a stop of even 100 pips or more, but often targeting hundreds of points in profit. The bottom line is ALWAYS HAVE A STOP that suits your trading style – and only YOU know what to do.

Lastly, DON'T TRADE MONEY THAT YOU CAN'T AFFORD TO LOSE!

Take a break

If you do have a streak of losing trades then shut the computer, take a break and stop trading for the rest of the day. Yes, you may end up losing an opportunity, but you are far more likely to save yourself from losses.

Also during the day, take lots of breaks, drink lots of water and trade in an environment with fresh air, do your stretches. I also meditate in between, and offer my prayers to God for making me successful. In fact my day in the office starts with prayers and listening to devotional music – once again this is what suits me and I have found success and relaxation. You have to do what suits you.

Stop Loss

Never, and I mean **NEVER EVER EVER** trade without a protective stop loss, this will apply to any trading strategy. Also if the position is moving against you, and you are close to your stop, do not move it, I personally have never moved my stop – that is breaking the first rule of discipline! – **NEVER DO IT!**

Don't Trade if you don't have to

When in doubt stay out! Key to higher profits is to have patience. Wait for a good trading setup. Markets are there every day – Trading for the sake of trading is plain stupid!

Be Flexible

Don't marry a trade. If you see that it is not going your way, be willing to change direction. When 'reasons' change or signals change – go with the change rather than insisting to go "your way".

Multiple Time Frames

At the start of the trading session, I always start looking at the longer time frames – taking a "big view" of the charts, drawing my trend lines and gradually moving down. Throughout each time frame I am looking for various chart patterns, this enables me to figure out the overall trend.

Trend Line Bounces

This is one of the easiest trading opportunities to spot, and to catch. If you see a nicely defined trend line, either UP or DOWN, look to catch the move once you have a confirmation. You can place your stop below the trend line or just below the previous low (for a long trade) or previous high for the short trade.

Trading Session Moves

Forex is one market, which trades 24 hours, apart from weekends, therefore even when you are asleep, the markets are moving. There are three major markets that trade FOREX;

The Asian market, including New Zealand and Australia
The European Market
North American Market.

Often the best moves to catch are the market overlap, i.e. Asian close and Europe open, and also the Europe afternoon and North American Open. Some trader's will only trade FOREX during these overlap periods, as these offer huge moves.

Fundamental News

Many "Forex Gurus" advise not to trade around or on the days of Fundamental News, for example the non-farm payroll days. I personally love the volatility, and if you catch the move, then probably you could achieve your week's target in just a few hours. Please refer to the main section covering the Fundamental News – where I discuss the trading opportunities.

What Kind of Trader are you?

No two traders have the exact same personality, bankroll or objectives. The first step in formulating a trading plan is to have a heart to heart with yourself and determine what kind of trading suits your unique character, funds and goals. Most traders fall into one of the following categories:

1. Day Trader – buys and sells very quickly, often times doing 10 or more trades each day; closes all positions by the end of each day.

2. Swing Trader – holds positions for bigger moves and a longer period of time than day traders; holding period is generally hours to days.

3. Long-Term Trader – holds positions for long periods of time, normally weeks to months.

There are trading strategies in this manual to suit all traders, in my case the day trader does not suit my personality and trading style, but I have been extremely successful using options 2 and 3. I have successfully held on to a position for weeks, through many FA's, finally coming out with a profit target of 500 pips! – How many day trades will I have to do to make 500 pips?

Daily Loss

Within your Trading Plan you should have a maximum daily loss limit. This is not for me to tell you, but you have to have a limit, which meets with your risk attitude and size of the Capital. Most traders will work with 2% of Capital; I have known some traders to work with 5%. You should be disciplined to take action and STOP trading once your limit has been reached. Often I have seen people try to get it back – only to lose more!

Give time for your trades to work

Be patient with winning trades. Don't look for excuses to take profit, use trailing stops based upon a systematic formula for locking in profits.

Forex Trend

Trade active currencies and only when significant price change is occurring: Trade in the direction of the tend, Do not try and be clever and fight the trend, listen to the market. Currencies trend very well, sometimes when they are in a trend, it may be worth hundreds of pips.

Traders Trend

Just like the trending market, you as a trader will also have a trend. You will also have an UP trend and a DOWN trend. When your trend is up, trade aggressively and when it's down, tread lightly. Take it easy when there is a trend change.

Trend

Don't try to enter the market tops or the bottoms, allow the trend to gain a foothold and then join the move. Follow the market wherever it wants to go, don't waste your time predicting where it will go.

Get used to fundamental News

When the Fundamental News is released, often it creates a move much greater than the news itself. You should get used to it. Often the markets may do totally opposite to what you expect, and jump hundreds of pips within minutes. That's why I say markets can be crazy.

KISS

Keep it simple. The more indicators the more ambiguity.

Target 20

When you are just starting out in Forex, initially aim to achieve a target of 20 pips, or closing at least half of your position for 20 pips. By having many lots of 20 pips profit will boost your confidence levels. Once you become a master trader you can set your eyes on bigger targets.

Stops for Insurance Purposes

This does not mean that you should snatch your profits, in order to protect profits you can employ a trailing stop.

Which Time Frame to use?

I often see many traders using 1 minute and 5 minute charts, in my view there is simply too much noise. I would only use this when there is huge volatility. Otherwise you want to focus on a 15 minute chart. Also look at the hourly chart to get an overall picture. Obviously, if you are looking to hold positions overnight or for few days, then you must regularly review the daily and even weekly charts.

MACD

MACD is a lagging indicator, and in my opinion is a useless indicator as a trigger. I mostly use MACD for divergences to make a trading decision. When the divergence strategy is used in conjunction with the Pivot levels, trend lines and Candle formations – This can be one of the most powerful triggers.

Become an expert

When you are starting out, I would strongly recommend that you pick one currency pair and get to know its patterns and how it behaves. Once you feel that you have more experience, then start to look other currency pairs.

Trading Journal

Whenever you trade, always make a record of all your trades, and learn from it. Analyse the trades – both profitable as well as losing trades and learn from them.

Trade the trend

Currencies trend very well, and often the trend could last for hundreds of pips. So have patience, don't buy too soon in a downtrend and don't sell too soon in an uptrend. If the trend is DOWN than think down, sell rallies, don't look to buy.

Look at the wider time scale

I would always recommend that you take a step back from the intraday action, and start having a look at longer chart time frames, i.e. 4 hours, daily or weekly charts. You will see these charts will offer up a clue as to where the prices are likely to go next.

Be Patient

Don't trade if you do not see any set-ups, don't just pull the trigger because you think it's time to do so, wait for the signal.

15 Minute Charts

Be sure to draw the Pivots and Fibonacci points, you can also draw trend lines. When prices break a trend at a juncture with a pivot or Fibonacci point, this could be very powerful evidence that the price is going the other way.

Your Psychology

For new traders to Forex, your confidence will grow as you have more winning trades, no matter how many – and of course cutting your losses. You will always have a losing trade – but don't beat yourself, learn from it, forget it and then move on. Don't try and be clever and second guess the tops and bottoms – believe in your system, and let it issue a signal and then take action.

Never listen to anyone, make your own decision based on your system, close your ears when you are trading, *STAY AWAY FROM NEGATIVE PEOPLE, BECAUSE THEY WILL DRAG YOU DOWN*. Focus on your success, for this will lead you to greater success. Be careful what you think about, as your thoughts will mould your actions and outcomes.

"The more I practice, the luckier I get"

Wayne Gretzky

Meditation / Relaxation

Traders love patterns – chart patterns, oscillator patterns and historical patterns, but Traders always lose sign of one pattern that is crucial and that is their emotional pattern when they trade. Successful trading requires an elimination of emotions. Traders can learn to become their own therapist – just how can you do this to help you?

I have noticed that ever since I started relaxation and meditation, my trading record has improved significantly. I spend at least 20 minutes each day in meditation, also take time off from trading to relax and also go to the gym. Don't get glued to your monitors for too long.

Repetition is mother of all skills

The more you practice good trading skills and disciplines, the better you will get. You have to keep at it, persistence is the key.

"Don't pick the top or the bottom is what most text books say, but I believe the most profits are made when the market turns at the top or the bottom. – You just got to know how to do it, when to do it!"

Jayendra Lakhani

SUMMARY & ACTION POINTS

1.) Review your trading for the past 12 months, what would you do differently and why?

2.) Why are you committed to make the change?

3.) What will be the consequences if you do not make the change?

PART 2

YOUR TRADING SYSTEM

CHAPTER 21
TECHNICAL ANALYSIS
CHART PATTERNS

- **Approach to Technical Analysis**

- **Support and Resistance**

- **Trend Lines**

- **Candle Sticks Charting**

- **Triangles**

- **Flags & Pennants**

- **Channel Breakouts**

- **Double Tops**

- **Double Bottoms**

- **Head and Shoulder Patterns**

- **Forex 1-2-3 pattern**

TECHNICAL ANALYSIS

"An approach to forecasting prices which examines patterns of price change, rates of change, and changes in volume of trading and open interest, without regard to underlying fundamental market factors."

FUNDAMENTAL ANALYSIS seeks to determine future stock price by understanding and measuring the objective "value" of equity. The study of stock charts, known as TECHNICAL ANALYSIS, believes that the past action of the market itself will determine the future course of prices.

Chartists study the market action, and will try and spot chart patterns, which repeat themselves. The goal is to profit from patterns that recur again and again. The chart shows the price action of the commodity, and it projects the hopes and fears of traders – that's what makes a market.

In order to succeed in trading, you need to listen to the market; it will tell you where it is going, so you can jump on the ride. Why use Charts? It plots the price action that has occurred in the past, and it will project the hopes and fears onto the charts. Smart money tends to put on trades when markets are quiet and may have bottomed whereas the amateur trader will tend to trade the news. The following chart on the GBP/USD perfectly illustrates this.

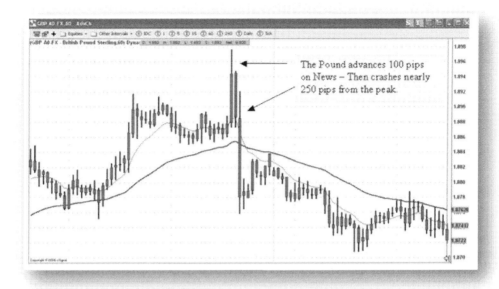

The Pound advances 100 pips on News – Then crashes nearly 250 pips from the peak.

As you can see from the above chart, a picture is worth a thousand words. In order to know where the price is going, we have to know where the price has been. Knowing if a market is moving up or down helps investors to make an informed decision whether to go long or short.

The chart simply shows the current crowd psychology, the analysis of the past price action can be used to forecast future price action. Technical Analysis is not always right, nothing is. Therefore to succeed you have to have a sound money management plan – cutting losses and letting profits ride.

SUPPORT AND RESISTANCE

Support is when price stops going down, and resistance is when price stops going up. Chart patterns are bound by support and resistance levels.

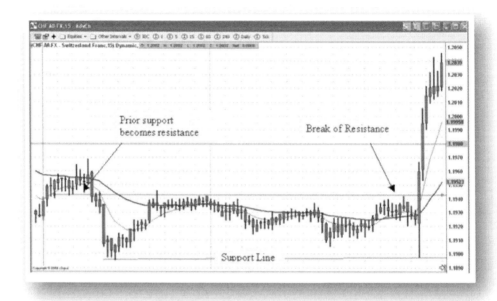

Source: eSignal. www.eSignal.com

In the above chart for CHFUSD, you can see that there had been a trading range, as soon as there is a break, the price has followed in the direction of the break.

After a market forms a pattern, it eventually starts a new trend higher or lower, a breakout occurs when the price moves through the support or resistance. This is called a BREAKOUT; this is perfectly illustrated in the above example.

TREND

Technical analysis attempts to gauge the strength and direction of a trend, once the trend is in motion it will continue in that direction for some time. Once the trend is determined early, the trend can be followed and more profit can be made.

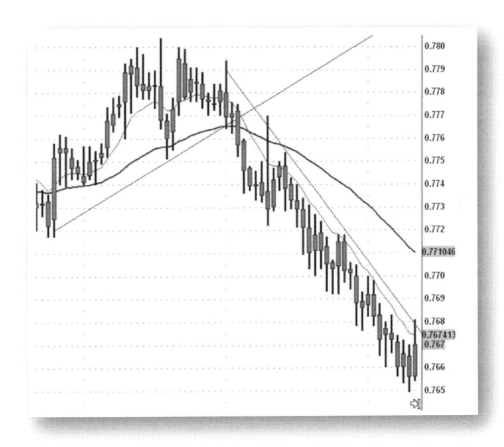

Source: eSignal. www.eSignal.com

The trend is your friend - Never fight a trend. In the above example of AUDUSD, the break of up trend is followed by a long down trend. The topping of price action is followed by a price break. Apart from high volatility in the Forex market, you will also notice that it also trends well – both giving perfect opportunities to make money.

167

The markets can only move in one of three ways; up, down, or sideways. That's it. Prices however do not move in a straight line, they move by zig-zagging up-down-up-down, so you will have-

An up trend

A downtrend, and

A sideways movement

These trends are illustrated in the following chart.

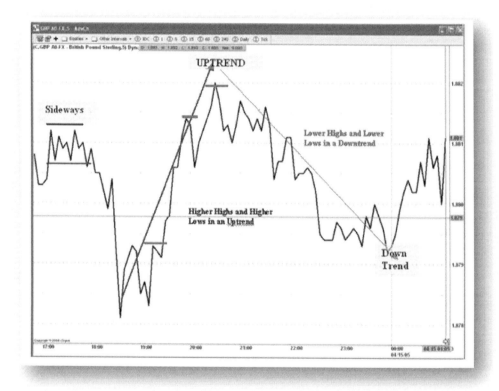

Source: eSignal. www.eSignal.com

Trends happen when traders worldwide believe that a price is either too low – so you will now be in an uptrend as you have buying pressure, or traders feel that the prices are too high – so you will be in a down trend as there is selling pressure. Sideways movement happen when traders either believe that the current price is more or less right, or when they are undecided. This normally happens when there is major news pending, for example prior to release of say Non Farms Payroll data.

The FOREX market trends very well, and that is the main reason why traders love FOREX. If all you knew was how to follow trends properly, then this alone could make you a very nice income. As they say, "A trend is your friend" or "never go against a trend!" The trend line is the most basic technical analysis, and all traders use it. It is amazing how price repeatedly bounces off the trend line.

An uptrend will have a series of higher highs and higher lows, whereas a downtrend will have a series of lower highs and lower lows. When you draw a trend line, whether an uptrend or a downtrend, so long as prices keep bouncing off the trend line you can keep making money. All trends will eventually end. A good indication that the trend is ending is when the price significantly penetrates through the trend line and takes out the previous low (up trend) or the high (downtrend).

CANDLE CHARTING BASICS

"A good beginning is the most important of things." (Japanese proverb)

Candlestick charts are much more visually appealing than a standard two-dimensional bar chart. Candles can represent any time frame. The four elements necessary to construct a candle chart are the OPEN, HIGH, LOW and CLOSING price for a given period. Below are the Examples of Candlestick and a definition for each candlestick component.

BULLISH CANDLE

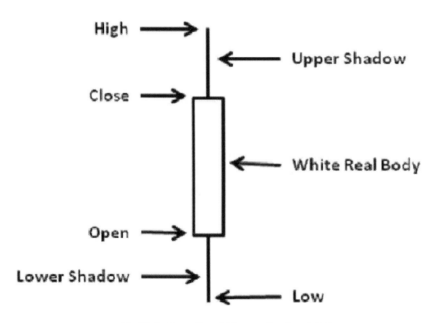

Bullish Candle - Prices closing higher

The above represents when prices close higher for that particular time frame, so will usually be green or light coloured.

BEARISH CANDLE

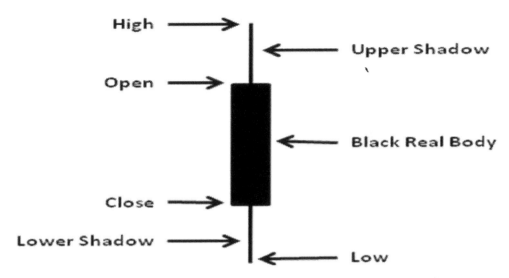

Bearish Candle - Showing prices closing lower than the open

The above candle represents when prices close lower for that particular time frame, so will usually be RED to dark.

You will come across probably hundreds of candle patterns, but I like to concentrate on a few of the most important ones that really work!

HAMMERS / HANGING MAN

Hammer with Bullish engulfing   Hanging man with Bearish engulfing

Hammers are formed after declines and hanging man after advances. When confirmed they become very powerful reversal signals.

HAMMERS / HANGING MAN - Example

HAMMER

This chart of CHF / USD perfectly illustrates a Hammer, which comes at the end of a downtrend. There is a large Lower Shadow and a small body. This is followed by a positive candle. You can see that the price action resulted into a big uptrend.

DOJI

Dojis are powerful reversal indicating candlesticks formed when security opens and closes at the same level, implying indecision in the price. Dojis become more significant, if seen after an extended rally of long bodied candles (bullish or bearish), and is confirmed by the engulfing candle, i.e. a long candlestick formed over the next period that engulfs the doji body.

Dojis can become support or resistance, usually on a short-term basis, a series of doji lines after a prolonged move could signal a rare and important top or bottom, an example of DOJI formation in the following chart

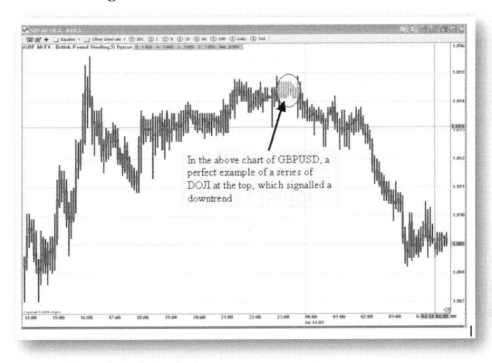

In the above chart of GBPUSD, a perfect example of a series of DOJI at the top, which signalled a downtrend

In the above chart, prior to a series of Dojis, there was a topping formation at around 1.8950, as you had a series of tops – Resistance.

The Dojis were followed by a trend line break, and a series of lower highs. Once again highlighting the importance of reading the chart patterns in conjunction with other signals and indicators.

SHOOTING STAR

The shooting star is made up of one candlestick (White or Black), with a small body, long upper shadow and small or non existent lower shadow, If this is followed by a down candle, there is a high probability of a downtrend, and may provide a good shorting opportunity.

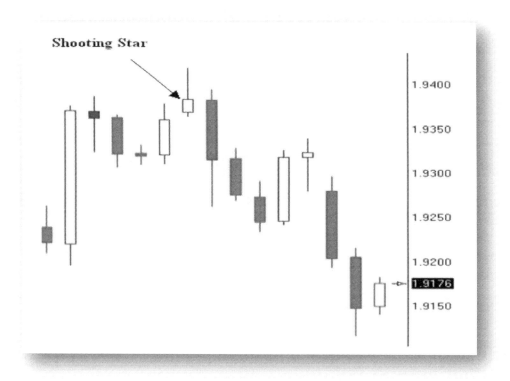

In this example, based on a 4-hour chart, the shooting star is followed by an extremely bearish candle. Overall this resulted in a move of over 250 pips over the next few periods. One can look for a better shorting entry by magnifying to a lower time frame chart, such as a 60-minute or 15 minutes.

TRIANGLE CHART PATTERNS.

Triangles frequently occur in the market, and this is a good way to catch some nice price moves. There are some traders who trade and focus ONLY on "triangle chart patterns" – and make handsome profits.

Symmetrical Triangles

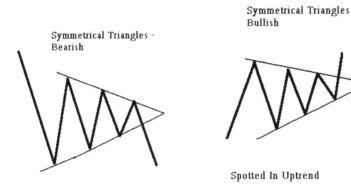

Symmetrical triangles are areas of indecision. Each top and bottom becomes shallow, as attempts to push the prices higher are quickly met by selling; eventually the price explodes out of this formation.

Ascending Triangle.

Ascending triangles are generally a bullish chart pattern, and most reliable when found in an up-trend. The top part of the triangle appears flat, while the bottom part is upward moving, with higher lows. Prices eventually break the flat top, which was the previous resistance. When this happens, the price may move considerably higher.

Ascending Triangle

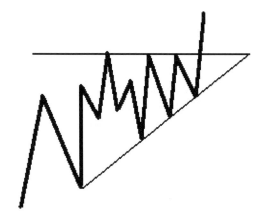

Flat top and Higher Lows -
Mostly break upside

Descending Triangle.

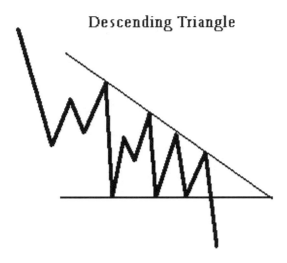

Descending Triangle

Flat Bottom and Lower Highs
Mostly Break down side

The Descending triangle is generally considered bearish. The bottoms are flat – offering support, whereas the highs are getting lower, as higher prices attract more sellers, and the price retests the old lows. Once again a good opportunity to trade the breakout.

FLAGS and PENNANTS

Flags and pennants are short-term continuation patterns that mark a small consolidation before the previous move resumes. These patterns are usually preceded by sharp advance or decline.

FLAGS

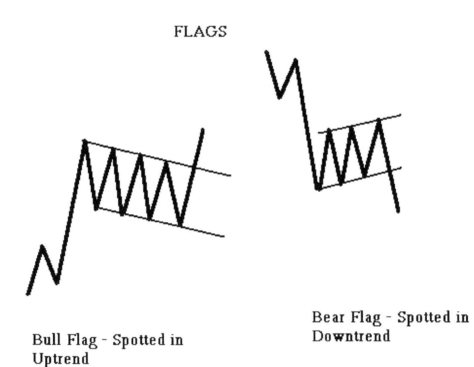

Bull Flag - Spotted in Uptrend

Bear Flag - Spotted in Downtrend

PENNANTS

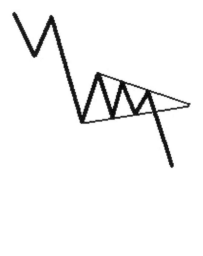

Pennants in Bullish
Trend

Pennants in Bearish
Trend

Pennants look very much like symmetrical triangles.

Channel Breakout

A Channel is formed between parallel support and resistance lines. This pattern usually indicates a strong trend, up, down or sideways is underway, until a breakout occurs.

Rectangles

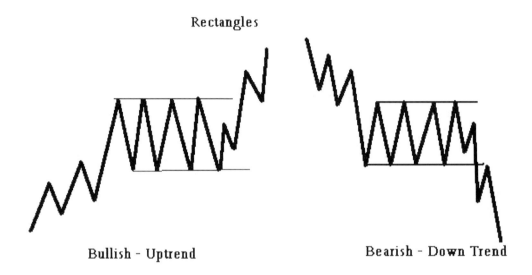

Bullish - Uptrend

Bearish - Down Trend

Trading Double Tops and Double Bottoms.

No chart pattern is more common in trading than a double bottom or double top. In fact this pattern appears so often that it alone may serve as a proof that price action is not wild. Price charts simply express trader sentiments. If price were truly random, then why do they pause so frequently at those points? The bulls and the bears defend these levels therefore generating strong profitable countermoves.

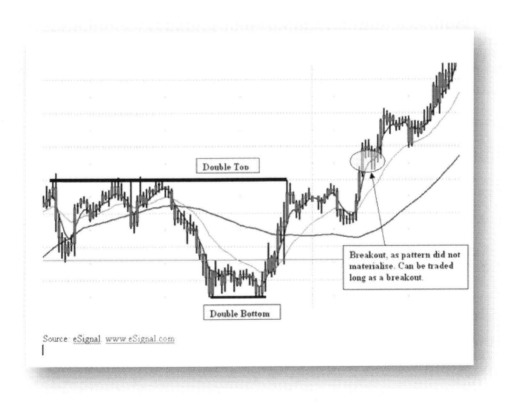

Source: eSignal www.eSignal.com

Head and Shoulders Pattern

The "Head-and-Shoulders" pattern is a trend reversal pattern. It marks the end of an up trend. Two lower peaks, or shoulders surround the "head". The neckline is drawn through the lowest points of the two shoulders, and may slope upward or downward

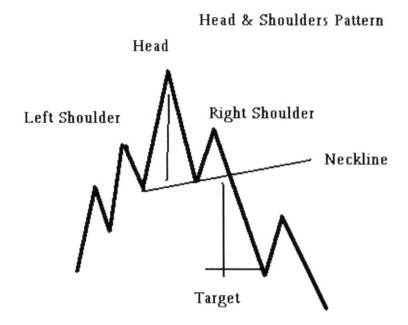

The reason this pattern could be a reversal is due to the fact that there appears to be a momentum of falling prices. The prices fail to make a higher low, the retracement from the head is likely to result in a break in the trend line, which has acted as a support. The markets attempts to move up, but only results in a lower high.

The target is calculated by measuring vertically from the highest point to the neckline, it is then projected down from the breakout. Once you identify the head & shoulder pattern, how would you manage your longs? You could consider to sell outright, and consider shorts at the break of neckline, tighten your stops so that your profits are locked in, or sell some of the position and hold the rest with tight stops. Your decision depends on how you feel about the pattern.

If you did not have any position, then you may want to consider a short when the neckline is broken, and place a stop above the previous high. Once again it would make sense to trade in conjunction with other indicators of your choice.

FOREX 1-2-3 METHOD

The 1-2-3 pattern is a reversal pattern and can be a very useful indicator to pick up the tops and bottoms. For maximum profit the 1-2-3 technique must be used as part of confluence of indicators, especially with the following methodologies;

- EMA Crossover system

- MACD & RSI Divergence system

- Break of RSI Trend line

This technique has been around for a long time, unfortunately not many traders use it correctly. Let's start with the basic concept. During any market trend, markets will retrace on a regular basis as they do not move in a straight line.

Often the first danger signs that the trend may be coming to an end is when the price fails to create a higher high in an uptrend and is followed by a lower low. So for example a bearish 123 setup is a LOWER HIGH in an uptrend; and a bullish 123 setup is a HIGHER LOW in a downtrend.

Here is a typical 1-2-3 setup in a Bear market as well as in a Bull market:

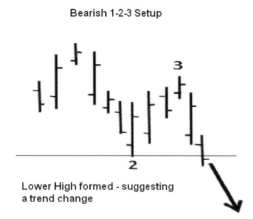

Bearish 1-2-3 Setup

Lower High formed - suggesting a trend change

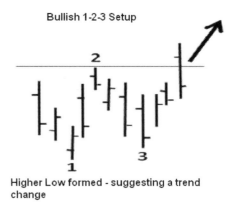

Bullish 1-2-3 Setup

Higher Low formed - suggesting a trend change

In a bearish 1-2-3 move you will often have a series of LOWER HIGHS and LOWER LOWS, whereas in a bullish 1-2-3 move the opposite is true. You have HIGHER HIGHS and a HIGHER LOWS.

On a breakout of point 2 on each of the above chart setups could result in a bigger move.

The following chart on GBPUSD is a good example of the 1-2-3 setups.

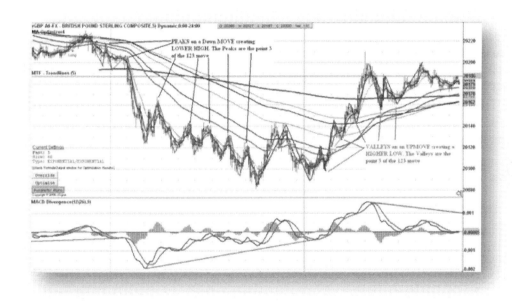

HOW TO TRADE USING 1-2-3?

The setup looks nice and simple; it should be used in conjunction with another methodology rather than stand alone. For example you could be using a divergence setup or an EMA crossover system. The entry point will be based on a 1-2-3 system.

When to enter?
Entry can be just after the Point 3, i.e. you are looking for a break of a trend line from points 2-3. Your stops to be around 15 pips below point 1. Once in a trade continue to monitor and manage

the trade. If there are good confluence of indicators at the entry point at the break of the 2-3 trend line, then there is a very high probability that the price will breakout at point 2.

Aggressive traders can add to their position on a breakout at point 2, or even on a retest of breakout at 2, thus creating a new 1-2-3 setup after the breakout.

So an example of a LONG trade using a divergence setup

1. Is the divergence setup confirmed?

2. Are the rules for the divergence trade met? (to be discussed in a later chapter)

3. Do you have a break of an overall trend line resistance?

4. After the trend line breakout do you have a retracement (point 2 of a 1-2-3 setup)

5. Do you have a trend line break between the points 2-3 of a 1-2-3 setup?

6. Is MACD in a BUY mode?

If you have YES to all the above points then you can enter a long trade. Here is an example of a divergence trade setup using the 1-2-3 system.

On the above example a 100 pip move using the 1-2-3 setup, after a divergence.

Another example of using a 1-2-3 setup using a bearish Divergence;

Looking at the above chart, we had lot of confluence of indicators;

1. Bearish Divergence

2. Break of trend line resistance

3. A 1-2-3 setup

4. Fibonacci retracement

5. Break of dynamic EMA supports

6. Trending 13 ema on a breakout
   MACD in sell mode

The above illustrates the power of a 1-2-3 setup, when used in conjunction with another trading system. It virtually guarantees a profitable trade.

CHAPTER 22

POWERFUL TRADING STRATEGIES

- Introductions – Trading Strategies

- Moving Averages

- MACD

- MACD Divergence Trading

- Relative Strength Index (RSI)

- Pivot Points

- Fibonacci

- Fundamental Announcements

INTRODUCTION: TRADING STRATEGIES

For a modern day trader a computer is a must. You are able to look at a number of complex technical Indicators which can be used as part of your day-to-day trading and managing your positions. Just like a majority of car drivers, you do not need to understand how the engine works, indeed many car drivers would even struggle to change a wheel, yet they have been driving for years.

My advice to many traders is to focus on the indicators and know how to read them, as opposed to what the indicators are and what their formula is and trying to work out the formula! Why invent a wheel, or indeed why change something if it works!

I come across so many traders, with so many ifs and buts. They are constantly looking to prove the author or the coach wrong, in the process burning so much of their precious energy in just trying to prove a point! Clearly such people will NOT succeed in life, let alone Trading!

There are several good quality charting packages available. To be successful, you have to invest in quality charting packages – whilst there are so many free charts you can get on the internet, many may have limitations.

Quality software will also allow you to write your indicators into the system and be able to edit some of the regular indicators that are already in the system. You are also able to back test your indicators, thus giving you some confidence on how you can apply it to live data, which is critical when you want to pull the trigger.

Indicators

Indicators will help you identify trends and reversal points, and will give you a better insight into the balance of power between bulls and bears. Indicators are more objective than chart patterns.

A good trader needs to know which indicator works in which market condition, you must understand what it measures and how it interacts with the price action. Most Traders divide indicators into:

Trend Following Indicators

These include moving averages, MACD, MACD Histogram. These indicators are lagging indicators and turn after trends reverse.

Oscillators

To help to identify turning points, they include stochastic, RSI and momentum. Oscillators, often turn ahead of prices.

The secret of successful trading is to combine several indicators from different groups, with chart patterns. I have found many traders who just concentrate on one indicator, which I feel is very dangerous, as often you can end up with a false signal.

Basic Theory

The most profitable way of trading the Forex market is to identify the trend and once it is identified, stay with it for as long as possible. Often you see the so-called Forex Gurus advising to take 20/30 pip profits, yet you could be at a start of a big move. Clearly with good money management and a trailing stop loss, you should be able to catch the big move.

Many traders, new to the Forex market end up overtrading, trying to enter the markets too often, and in my early days I was not an exception, often incorrectly identifying a trend.

A fisherman cannot catch a fish every day, so too a Forex trader cannot catch a trade every day. You have to have patience and only trade if your system tells you to do so. If there is no trade, don't trade – is a simple rule. Markets are there every day, and opportunities will come, however if you desperately try to find a trade when none exists, than this will only frustrate you. One of the most important lessons I can teach you is patience.

Often I see that new traders having an incorrect entry point, this is equally followed by an incorrect placement of a stop loss. Most have been taught to place no more than a 20 point stop loss, and also just around the previous support/resistance. How often have you seen stops that have been gunned down, and then the market continues to go in the direction you first thought it would. Your entry point, stop loss and exit levels must all be logical and must be able to produce you consistent profits.

Incorrect placement of a stop loss can sometimes result in being stopped out just at a reversal point. Have a look at the following example-

A signal for a short entry, price level was at 1.9050, signals for the short entry were:

1. Macd divergence

2. RSI Divergence

3. Resisting at R1

4. Resisting at a Pivot level

If say you had a 20 or 25 pip, the position would have been stopped out. The cable peaked at 1.9076, briefly consolidated, and then it eventually fell by over a 100 pips from its peak.

GBP /USD

Enter Short at 1.9050

Source: eSignal. www.eSignal.com

I hear a lot of so called "gurus" in various books and trading
seminars advising on a 20 pip stop loss. With so much of
volatility, Forex can move 20 pips in minutes if not seconds, and if
you were on the wrong side of a trade, you are stopped out. Most
of them also recommend not to trade unless the risk reward is 1
to 3 and above. I am simply baffled by this advice.

To be honest a lot of these guys are not traders themselves. One
Guru at a trading seminar says "only morons will trade with a risk
reward of 1 to 1, and adds that a trader should only risk £25 to
make £100 – a risk reward of 1 to 4 – looks great on paper, and
yes the books and trading seminars will sell like hot cakes! In my
opinion in most cases the risk/reward ratio is a lie. It is a fun
fantasy. Often an amateur sets unrealistic stops and lowers risks
to reward, but ends up being stopped out and never achieving the
profit target.

What is important is that you are able to steadily increase your Capital, if that means having a risk reward of 1:1 or 1:2, then so be it. Of course, once you get experienced and can read the market accurately, then even a risk reward of 1:10 is possible. On some of my swing trading positions, this has often been achieved.

However, when I am trading intraday, having done my research and I am reasonably sure of the direction of the trend, I am not at all concerned in having a tight 20 pip stop loss. I would rather lose 60 pips on a well thought out trade with a good market direction, than lose 3 lots of 20 pips trying to achieve the same thing. That does not mean I cannot have tight stops, there have been many instances where there could be a finely balanced trade, and the market could go either way. I have even gone in with a 10 pip stop loss. You have to be flexible, and the market direction should dictate where to put the stop loss.

In fact, if I was trading a shorter time frame, I would often start with a risk reward of 1 to 1, what I focus on is having the least number of trades that get stopped out. Generally, I am able to get a winning percentage of 70%, 7 winning trades (7x60 = 420 pips) 3 losing trades (3x60 = 180 pips) – that still gives me a net profit of 240 pips!

Thank you, I would rather have that instead of so many losing trades of 20 pips!

Which Time Frame to Use

When I first started trading Forex, I was taught to look at 1 & 5 minute charts, have a stop loss of 20 pips and a target of 20 pips. The majority of my trades would be stopped out and few would have been profitable. Profits were snatched too early, some of those winning trades had offered an opportunity to bank not 20 pips but more than 50 or 100 pips.

It was only after I started using the larger time frame that I realised that the Support and Resistance were more relevant on say a 60 minute chart than a 1 minute or 5 minute chart.

On my screen I will look at four time frames, which would be 15 min, 1 hour, 4 hour and daily. You could use any combination, which suits your trading style, this would be -

Tick, 1 minute, 5 minute, and 15 minute
5 minute, 15 minute, 30 minute and 60 minute etc

In this situation, you are able to see the trend in the larger time frame, which will enable you to pin point your entry and exit levels.

Take a look at the image below and see what my screen usually looks like.

Source: eSignal. www.eSignal.com

I would use the above format if I were looking for a trade using macd divergence, as you can see I have a 4 screen layout, a 15 min, 60 min, 4 hour, and a daily chart.

At the time of writing this book, the system issued a short signal on the EURJPY. As you can see there was a MACD divergence (to be explained later) first on a daily chart, then followed by a divergence on the 4-hour chart. Seeing this signal on 2 charts gives you more confidence to pull the trigger, together with the moving average system (discussed later) that I use.

Having seen this divergence, I would then turn to 60 min and 15 min charts to look for a better entry. Trigger pulled and short at 139.62. Currently the price is 135.60 – that is a profit of 402 pips and I'm still in the trade.

The 15 min charts are turning bullish, but a strong resistance at 135.80, so my stops have been moved to 136.20. However, looking at the 4-hour and daily chart, you can see that we are still in a strong down trend. It is this market direction that has kept me in the trade.

The market direction has kept me in the position on the short side from an open entry level of 139.62. Stop losses are continually being moved to lock in the profits.

MOVING AVERAGE CROSSOVER TRADING STRATEGIES

Introduction

There are three types of moving averages: simple, exponential and weighted. Moving averages are one of the most popular and easy to use tools available to the technical analyst. They smooth out the price action and therefore it makes it easier to spot a trend, and this is particularly helpful in volatile and trending markets. They also form the building blocks for many other technical indicators and overlays.

A moving average is the composite photograph of the market – it combines prices for several days. The market consists of huge crowds, and the moving average identifies the direction of mass movement.

It must be noted that all moving averages are lagging indicators and will always be behind price. Currencies trend very well, so they fit well with trend following indicators. When prices are trending, moving averages work very well. I have often used the crossover of Exponential Moving Averages (EMA). This strategy will not work well in a sideways market, as there will be numerous false signals. In order to reduce the lag in simple moving averages, I tend to use the EMA.

Exponential Moving Averages (EMA)

EMA is better at trend following than a simple MA. It gives greater weight to the latest data and responds to changes faster than a simple MA. A successful trader does not forecast the future – he monitors the market and manages his trading position. Moving averages will help us trade in the direction of the trend.

No doubt there are literally hundreds of variations on various trading systems using the crossovers of moving averages to initiate a trading position. One of my favourites is the use of 5, 20 and 60 period EMA. Like all other mechanical trading methods, this will work well in a strongly trending market.

The system that I have successfully used is based on the following rules-

1.) USE a 5, 20 and 60 PERIOD EMA For ENTRY.

2.) USE a 13 EMA as a dynamic support/resistance and also to monitor your trade.

3.) USE a 200 and 610 periods EMA as a very strong indication of market strength. So if prices are above the 200 ema the emphasis is on the long side and if below the 200 ema then the emphasis is on the short side.

Warning to Buy

When the 5 EMA crosses the 20 EMA moving UPWARD. This indicates that the currency pair is likely to reverse into an up trend.

Confirmation to Buy

When the 5 EMA crosses the 60 EMA moving upward, it indicates that the currency is on an up trend momentum.

Warning to sell short

This is the exact opposite of the buy signal, When the EMA5 crosses the EMA20 moving downward, this indicates that the currency pair may be in a downtrend, so be ready to short and continue to monitor the price action.

Confirmation to sell short

This is when the EMA5 crosses the EMA60 moving downwards, this would indicate that the currency is in a downtrend.

RULES FOR ENTRY ORDER – <u>LONG</u> EMA Crossover

1.) Is there an EMA Crossover of 5/60?   MOVING UP
2.) Do you have support? This is to assess the risk, because if there is no significant support close to entry then this would become a high risk trade.
3.) Has there been a break of resistance? (Trend line, Other EMA, Pivots etc)
4.) After the break of RESISTANCE is there a 1-2-3 pattern?
5.) On the 1-2-3 pattern, is there a break of 2-3 trend line?
6.) Is MACD above the waterline?

If the answer is YES to all of the above points, pull the trigger.

Risk Management

1.) Entry on a break of 2-3 line.
2.) Stops at least 15-30 pips below a support.
3.) Break the position into at least 2 portions.
4.) Take incremental profits (Scale down winners) aim to close the first portion for 20 – 30 pips.Your Take Profit 1 target should ideally be same as your stop loss, so TP2 enjoys a free ride.
5.) Aim to close the 2nd portion for 50-75 pips.
6.) Alternatively, Let the final portion run until the signal reverses.
7.) Trail the stop loss to 30 pips below the 60 EMA or 13EMA.
8.) Don't wait to be stopped out. If the signal reverses or the price is not doing what you expect it to do, then close the trade. The golden rule must be to keep the losses small and winners big!

If however, there is an aggressive price action, following the crossover of EMA, then you may wish to consider a market order to fill your trade. Because currencies trend well, therefore, you will be able to catch a bigger move.

RULES FOR ENTRY ORDER - SHORT

1.) Is there an EMA Crossover of 5/60? MOVING DOWN

2.) Do you have RESISTANCE? This is to assess the risk, because if there is no significant resistance close to entry then this would become a high risk trade.

3.) Has there been a break of support? (Trend line, Other EMA, Pivots etc)

4.) After the break of support is there a 1-2-3 pattern?

5.) On the 1-2-3 pattern, is there a break of 2-3 trend line?

6.) Is MACD BELOW the waterline?

If the answer is YES to all of the above points, pull the trigger.

Risk Management

1.) Entry on a break of 2-3 line.

2.) Stops at least 15-30 pips ABOVE a resistance.

3.) Break the position into at least 2 portions.

4.) Take incremental profits (Scale down winners) aim to close the first portion for 20 – 30 pips.

5.) Let the final portion run until the signal reverses.

6) Trail the stop loss to 30 pips ABOVE the 60 EMA or 13EMA.

7.) Don't wait to be stopped out. If the signal reverses or the price is not doing what you expect it to do, then close the trade. The golden rule must be to keep the losses small and winners big!

GBP – Short Trade.

Source: eSignal. www.eSignal.com

The above trade at best could have produced a profit of 175 pips, having entered short at 1.8935 leading to the lowest point at 1.8760. I would let this trade run until I saw a significant turn on the 20 period EMA, the first such signal would have been at 1.8790, producing 145 pips, or the crossover of 20 period EMA with the 60 period EMA – this would have produced a profit of 125 pips. – Not a bad trade, but how many traders would have had patience to hold on to this trade!

Patience is the key – Wait for the signal, then let your profits run.

Source: eSignal. www.eSignal.com

Obviously when using the crossover of moving averages, you would also look at other signals in addition.

Just relying on one indicator is dangerous and risky.

If we look at the above chart, you have a double bottom, a higher low, then consolidates, then breaks out of the triangle pattern. This coincides with the EMA crossover.

When you have such confluence of events, the certainty of a profitable trade is much higher.

CHF – SHORT trade - DAILY CHART

Source: eSignal. www.eSignal.com

Using the Daily chart, a Short signal at 1.2601.

One could have taken profits at 1.1300, when there was a double bottom –that is a profit of 1300 pips. Would you have had patience to hold on to this trade for long? It is possible if you have a set of rules, which you follow strictly, of course you would have a trailing stop loss so that your profits are locked.

If you had waited for the turning of the 20 period moving average, you could have closed the trade at around 1.1500 – that still produced a profit of 1101 points!

If however, you had waited for the crossover of the 20 and 60 period crossover, that would have produced a gain of 800 pips, obviously chances are that you would have taken profits much earlier, using other signals, such as the double bottom.

This simple system can work on all time frames, as illustrated. Once again this illustrates that currencies trend well, and EMAs can be used to stay in the trade for as long as the trend is in your direction.

The longer the time frame means a longer wait and entry could result much later, resulting in missing out on a big move.

I would recommend the 3 min, 5 min, and 15 min time frame for Intraday trading. Use 30 min, 60 min and 4h charts for swing trading.

Ensure you follow the Rules as explained above.

In addition to the EMA crossover signals described above, you can also use the MACD (explained later) to confirm the trend. Always use the default settings of 12 and 26 to calculate the MACD on your charts.

There are 4 basic stages to this cycle;

1.) The MACD crosses the zero line moving upwards.

2.) The MACD continues to increase until it reaches the maximum value.

3.) The MACD then starts to decrease until it passes Zero.

4.) The MACD continues to decrease moving downward to the minimum value.

From the above, If MACD is in Phase 1, it verifies the confirmation of a buy signal, and if MACD is in phase 3 it verifies the confirmation to sell short.

See the following example-

Source: eSignal www.eSignal.com

Using the EMA crossover signal in conjunction with MACD means that the likelihood of a false signal is reduced, as illustrated in the above trade. As you can see that prior to the signal there were few trades where you would have been stopped out, as the markets were range bound.

Therefore once again, what you are looking for is a confluence of events.

An example of a Short Trade

GBP USD – Short at 1.8935

Source: eSignal. www.eSignal.com

A successful trader does not forecast the price action; he monitors the markets and manages his trading position. Moving averages are excellent indicators to work with when the markets are trending, so they help us to trade in the direction of the markets. Moving Averages work very well in a strongly trending market, however, when you see that the markets are not trending, i.e. they are trading sideways, then you will have many cases of whipsaws. Therefore when the markets trade in ranges, just stand aside and be patient until a new trend emerges.

The advantage of using moving averages in Forex is that the markets trend very well, it is not often you see very long sideways movement compared to Stocks.

Moving Averages lag market reversals at Top and bottoms, the larger the MA the longer the lag period, the shorter the MA the shorter the lag period, but more frequent the whipsaws.

MOVING AVERAGE CONVERGENCE DIVERGENCE (MACD)

Gerald Appel developed the MACD indicator and it is simply a method of identifying the potential for two exponential moving averages to cross. MACD is calculated using a short length and a long length exponential moving average (defaulted to 12 and 26) and calculating the difference between these two averages. In other words, it is the spread between the two averages. Normally, a signal line is derived by calculating an exponential moving average of the MACD. You can also have the MACD displayed as a histogram – a series of vertical bars above and below a zero line.

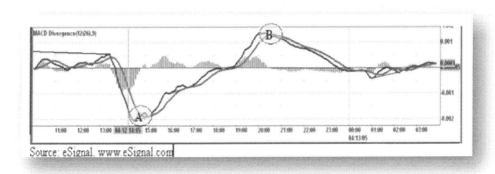

Source: eSignal, www.eSignal.com

Crossovers of the MACD and signal lines identify shifts in the balance of power of bulls and bears. Trading in the direction of a crossover means going with the flow of the market.

When the fast MACD line crosses above the slow signal line, it gives a buy signal. Go long, and place a protective stop below the latest low. **See A above**.

When the fast line closes below the slow line, it gives a sell signal. Go short and place a protective stop above the latest minor high. **See B above**.

MACD HISTOGRAM.

The MACD Histogram gives a more in-depth guide to the balance of power between bulls and bears, and tells us if the bulls and bears are getting stronger or weaker. In my opinion one of the best tools. In the above chart, you can see that just before point A, the bears are losing momentum.

MACD- HISTOGRAM and PRICE DIVERGENCES.

Divergences between MACD Histogram and prices identify major turning points. These signals do not occur often, but when they do, they often let you catch major reversals and the beginning of a new trend.

In my opinion the MACD divergence is probably the strongest signal in Technical Analysis. You could probably make a living trading the divergences only! MACD should be a copycat of the price action, and therefore macd will also make a higher high same as a price action, if this pattern is not repeated then you have a divergence.

When prices rally to a new high, but MACD traces lower, this is a bearish divergence, this shows that the bulls are getting weaker, this would identify a price weakness at market tops.

The following is an example of a Bearish Divergence.

Another example of a perfect MACD Bearish Divergence
A possible entry at 1.8670,

The EMA crossover at 1.8295 will still keep you in this trade; at this point the profit from the trade was 375 pips.

You could consider closing the position at 1.7970 when the 20 EMA starts to rise, this giving a profit of 700 pips.

At this stage the 20 EMA has not crossed over the 60 EMA, so some of you may want to carry on with the trade. If you did so then you would have had a perfect opportunity to close the trade at the Double bottom on 7/10/04 at 1.7760 – giving a total of 910 pips profit.

Not a bad trade, from divergence.

MACD BULLISH DIVERGENCE

If the prices fall to a new low but MACD traces a more shallow low, it would mean that bulls are ready to gain control, and this would identify strength at market bottoms. This is a Bullish divergence. They give buy signals when most traders feel fearful about a breakdown to a new low!

The following chart illustrates a perfect MACD Bullish divergence on a EURUSD Chart

Source: eSignal. www.eSignal.com

You could consider longs when the MACD Histogram ticks up from its shallower bottom; while prices are at a new low, place a protective stop below its latest low.

The higher the time frame of a chart in which the MACD divergence occurs, may result in a larger move.

216

For example in the above chart, at around 1.2250 the peak of that rally had been 1.2850 – thereby giving an overall gain of 600 pips. In this instance your entry points were much earlier than the EMA 5/60 day crossover.

All the above strategies will work in any time frame, so unlike me, if you enjoy the thrills and excitement of watching your screens for every second to catch 20 to 30 pips per trade, then you can certainly switch the charts to a lower time frame, i.e. 1 minutes or 5 minutes.

RULES FOR ENTRY ORDER – LONG BULLISH DIVERGENCE

1. Is there a Bullish divergence? Prices coming down and MACD going up.
2. Do you have support? This is to assess the risk, because if there is no significant support close to entry then this would become a high risk trade.
3. Has there been a break of resistance? (Trend line, Other EMA, Pivots etc)
4. After the break of RESISTANCE is there a 1-2-3 pattern?
5. On the 1-2-3 pattern, is there a break of 2-3 trend line?
6. Is MACD above the waterline?

If the answer is YES to all of the above points, pull the trigger.

Risk Management

1. Entry on a break of 2-3 line.
2. Stops at least 15-30 pips below a support.
3. Break the position into at least 3 portions.
4. Take incremental profits (Scale down winners) aim to close the first portion for 20 – 30 pips.
5. Let the final portion run until the signal reverses.
6. Trail the stop loss to 30 pips below the 60 EMA or 13EMA.
7. Don't wait to be stopped out. If the signal reverses or the price is not doing what you expect it to do, then close the trade. The golden rule must be to keep the losses small and winners big!

RULES FOR ENTRY ORDER FOR SHORT BEARISH DIVERGENCE.

1. Is there an Bearish Divergence? MOVING DOWN
2. Do you have RESISTANCE? This is to assess the risk, because if there is no significant resistance close to entry then this would become a high risk trade.
3. Has there been a break of support? (Trend line, Other EMA, Pivots etc)
4. After the break of support is there a 1-2-3 pattern?
5. On the 1-2-3 pattern, is there a break of 2-3 trend line?
6. Is MACD BELOW the waterline?
7. If the answer is YES to all of the above points, pull the trigger.

Risk Management

- Entry on a break of 2-3 line.
- Stops at least 15-30 pips ABOVE a resistance.
- Break the position into at least 3 portions.
- Take incremental profits (Scale down winners) aim to close the first portion for 20 – 30 pips.
- Let the final portion run until the signal reverses.
- Trail the stop loss to 30 pips ABOVE the 60 EMA or 13EMA.

Don't wait to be stopped out. If the signal reverses or the price is not doing what you expect it to do, then close the trade. The golden rule must be to keep the losses small and winners big!

Relative Strength Index (RSI)

The relative strength Index (RSI) is a momentum-based indicator. Determining the true value of an oscillator depends on the understanding of overbought or oversold positions. The basic formula for calculating RSI is as follows:

100-(100/(1+U/D)
U = average upward price change
D = average of downward price change

RSI as an indicator is front weighted i.e. it gives more importance to more recent price action. It gives a better velocity reading than other oscillators; it also tends to filter out lots of noise. Your software should be able to do the work for you.

On the RSI indicator there is a scale of 0 to 100, which indicates that the overbought position is at above 70 and oversold position is at below 30. Some traders use the 80/20 range, as they do not want to pull the trigger too fast!

Some traders also use the short term moving average crossovers, this will also indicate a shift in direction, and if this occurs when the RSI is at extreme levels then it could be a powerful set-up to pull the trigger.

There are 5 different uses for RSI;

1. Tops and bottoms – overbought and oversold conditions are usually signalled at 30 and 70.
2. Divergences – when a pair makes new highs or lows, but the RSI does not follow price action, this usually indicates that price reversal is coming.
3. Support and Resistance – RSI may show levels of support and resistance, same as the price chart itself.
4. Chart Formations – Patterns such as double tops and head and shoulder can also be very powerful on RSI as well
5. Failure swings – when RSI breaks out, i.e. it surpasses a previous high or low, this may indicate that a breakout in price is coming.

It is important to understand that an overbought or oversold position can remain in an extended up trend or downtrend for some time, so try and use other methods combined with RSI, rather than using it on its own.

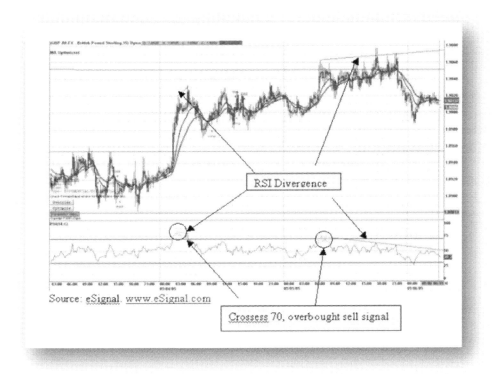

Source: eSignal, www.eSignal.com

RSI Divergence

Crossess 70, overbought sell signal

In the above chart, RSI was useful in detecting a short trade after a divergence and a crossover of the 70 "overbought" level. The above chart is in a 5-minute time frame. There are at least 2 good short trades.

On the long side, notice the RSI bouncing just around the 30 oversold, subsequently there is a double bottom, and a divergence on the RSI. This was around the price level 1.880.

Having a closer review of the above 5-minute chart, this covers a two-day period. The GBP has not moved much, yet there were a few opportunities to trade both from the long side as well as short, with a gain of more than 100 pips.

RSI TRENDLINE BREAK SYSTEM

The RSI trend line support/resistance break can be very profitable, if you were to follow just a simple set of rules, which are;

1. A break of the RSI line which goes from extreme to extreme, i.e. a break of the RSI line from 30 and 70 for shorts, and a break of RSI line from 70 and 30 for longs
2. This break in the RSI support & resistance lines can often result into a trend change.
3. This must also be followed by the price trend line break.
4. After the break look for a 1-2-3 setup, Look for confluences i.e. Retracement to Fibonacci, pivots etc.

Look for other confluence of indicators, i.e. Divergence, EMA crossover system.

I have highlighted 3 very profitable trades from the above chart. All were very good short trades. Can you spot any other trades?

Pivot Points as a Support and Resistance Tool

Pivot points are one of the primary tools used by many Forex Traders, and yet they are not commonly taught at Forex Courses, also the average trader does not generally understand them.

Using pivot points as a trading strategy has been around for a long time and was originally used by the floor traders. Pivot points can be calculated using a few simple arithmetic calculations, of the previous 24 hour "session" days high, low and close. A series of points are delivered. These points can be critical support or resistance levels. These Pivots are valid for the next 24 hours, and you have to calculate them on a daily basis.

Pivots are also widely used by the bank and institutional traders, where a large part of FOREX volume is based, so I guess they become accurate by definition. Since much of the volume on Forex depends on these techniques, pivot lines then become the focal points for the battles between buyers and sellers. Whilst no system is perfect, when a trading strategy is devised in conjunction with other indicators or chart formations, Pivot levels can become very powerful.

You can easily develop a Pivot calculator, using an Excel spreadsheet. One formula that is widely used is as follows-

Open Price
High
Low
Close

R3 $\quad\quad$ = High +2*(pivot – Low)
R2 $\quad\quad$ = Pivot +(R1 – S1)
R1 $\quad\quad$ = 2*Pivot – Low

PIVOT $\quad$ = (high + Close + Low) / 3

S1 $\quad\quad$ = 2*Pivot – High
S2 $\quad\quad$ = Pivot – (R1 – S1)
S3 $\quad\quad$ = Low – 2*(High – Pivot)

Most charting software does have an automatic pivot line plotted on the chart. From the above formula, you eventually finish with 7 points, 3 resistance levels, 3 support levels and the actual pivot point. In addition 2 other points are very important as well which are the previous day's high and the low. Often these would act as strong support or resistance points. But once they have been broken, often you will see a significant move up or down.

In determining when to enter a trade you will also look for the usual candlestick formations indicating reversals (Hammers, Railway Tracks, spinning tops etc). Confirmation with technical indicators such as RSI is also useful. Adding trend lines is also very important, as when you have confluence of events, you could expect a price explosion.

The three most important pivots are R1, S1 and the actual pivot point. The general idea behind trading pivots is to look for a reversal or break of R1 or S1. By the time the market reaches R2, R3 or S2, S3 the market will already be overbought or oversold and these levels should be used for exits rather than entries.

USDCAD – 27th April 2004

Short signal

Close your shorts and consider longs

On the above chart the Canadian Dollar was nicely trending up, pierces through R1, but is quickly followed by Railway Tracks in the next candle. If you were watching the charts, then you could have gone short at 1.2490. This is then followed by a crossover of moving averages. Sit back and enjoy the ride!

The downtrend stalls precisely around the pivot point! – Who could have guessed? It is unable to close decisively under the pivot point. After the Doji, the market turns higher, clearly time to close your shorts and consider longs. In the space of 2 hours a nice long and short trade, overall producing at least 100 pips.

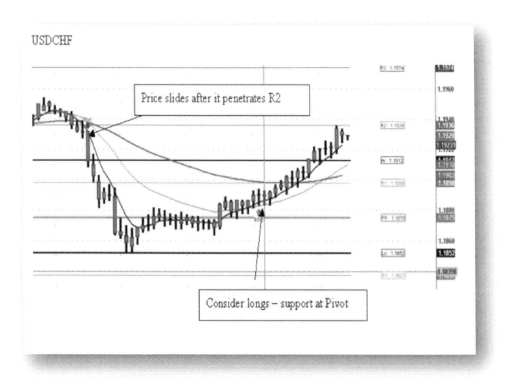

USDCHF

Price slides after it penetrates R2

Consider longs – support at Pivot

Another good Trade on the USDCHF on 27th April 2005.

Price pierces through R2 at 1.1936, followed by a doji then the slide began. On its way down it passes through R1, then the Pivot level at 1.1875, but stalls just short of S1. It now starts consolidating, but the pivot is now acting as a strong resistance. As soon as the Pivot is breached decisively, it now acts as a support. Guess it's time to close the shorts and consider longs, producing at least 60 pips.

On the way back up, look at the pattern, having gone through R1, it stalls precisely at R2 – who could have guessed! – Yet another trade producing 50 pips.

On the above examples I have not gone deeply into patterns around the pivot levels, or looked at other indicators, but that is not the point of this lesson. I just wanted to introduce another possible way for you to trade.

Fibonacci

Fibonacci is a massive subject and there are a lot of different areas you could investigate, however, for the purposes of the method to be used in this training material, we shall only be concentrating on a few specific points.

Leonardo Pisano (Nickname Fibonacci) was a mathematician, born in 1170, in Pisa, Italy. Fibonacci had also learnt accounting. Fibonacci contributed to the science of numbers, and introduced the ' Fibonacci sequence'.

The Fibonacci sequence is as follows:- 1,1,2,3,5,8,13,21,34,55,89,144 etc every next number is the sum of the preceding two.

There are also Fibonacci ratios, by comparing the relationship with each number, and each alternate number and even to the number which is four places to the right, we arrive at some fairly consistent ratios. The important ones are .236, .50, .382, .618, .764, 1.382 1.618, 2.618, 4.236.

For example if you divide 34 by 89 = 0.382. As a trader you do not need to go into the mechanics of working out the numbers, as your charting program will work all this out for you.

It turns out that the Fibonacci ratios are prevalent in nature around us, in the universe, in plants etc, so what you may ask do the Fibonacci techniques have to do with the trading environment?

Traders study the charts, and Fibonacci ratios can be applied to the price scale and time scale of the charts. Prices never move in a straight line, they advance then retrace, and if you normally look at the price patterns they tend to retrace in Fibonacci proportions often enough.

To determine the Fibonacci retracement;

- Determine a significant High to low price move or vice versa – Low to high.

- Using the charting software calculate the Fibonacci retracement points which would then be automatically plotted on your charts.

- Wait for the prices to retrace, and look for price action at or around the key Fibonacci points and look for confirmation.

- Look for confluence of indicators at the same level. The more support/resistance points at the same level and it can become a very important point. For example you could have a trend line resistance, a pivot, which also is a Fibonacci point, you may also have an EMA resistance. It then becomes more likely that the price may stall precisely at this level. If however there is a breakout, than expect a big move up.

Let us now have a look at some chart examples, looking for confluence of events at major Fibonacci points;

The above chart produced over a 200 pip move, after the price bounced off the 200 ema, which was also the 61.8% Fibonacci retracement point. Fibonacci just adds an edge to your trading.

Using Fibonacci & Pivot Points

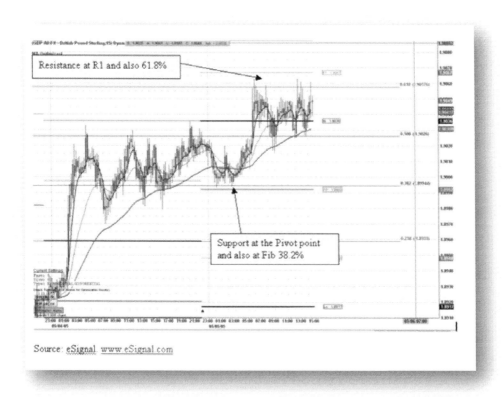

Source: eSignal www.eSignal.com

Have a look at the above chart – GBP/USD on 05th May 2005, on a day when there was not a great deal of price action, but trading within a channel.

Look at the way the price slide was halted at the Pivot point, which also coincided with the 38.2% Fibonacci level. Who would have guessed?

Having bounced from the 38.2% and pivot point, it is on a steady up trend, rising by 60 pips, but only to be stopped at Fibonacci 61.8%, which also coincided with R1.

Many attempts were made for higher prices, but the rally repeatedly stopped at R1 & 61.8%. Once again this further illustrated how you can have an easy trade when combining two or more studies together. On the above example, even though the cable moved only 60 pips, an active trader could have easily made over 100 pips – just trading off the pivot and Fibonacci levels, obviously with tight stops.

Do not blindly anticipate the market to turn at a Fib level. Support and resistance levels are there to be broken. It takes some skill to determine which Fib level is likely to cause the market to turn, therefore you should experiment with as many charts as possible. No technical study is perfect, you must develop the skills to filter out bad trades, and improve the odds of finding better trades.

Another example of CHF

On the above chart example on CHF, 4 hour chart, we had a 500 pip move, after the price retraced exactly to the 61.8% Fibonacci retracement. This level is also where there was other major resistance.

Fundamental Announcements
Looking at the calendar.

On the fundamental announcement (FA) days, you will see some extreme volatility, and this will sometimes offer you the best trading opportunities. This will result in the best breakout days, as sometimes the prices may move by 100 pips or more within a few minutes of announcements.

Keep an eye on the time when the numbers are being released. Release of key economic data seems to generate more price action than say speeches. It is really difficult to anticipate what will create strong reactions, but after practicing for some time you should get a feel of what to expect.

Always review the night before, the key fundamental announcements for the next day. Set your plan in advance and you should have better success. The time spent planning on such matters separates you from the novice traders, showing that you are a professional quality trader who takes time to properly plan your trades, and then trade your plan.

There are certain FAs that are much more likely to result in strong movements. If there is uncertainty about the announcement, then there will be a drastic effect on the Forex market. The most important to watch are ;

- Unemployment reports
- Interest rates
- Consumer price index (CPI)
- Inflation
- Gross Domestic Product (GDP)
- M2 Money supply
- Producer Price Index
- Various surveys – U. of Michigan confidence and the Tankan Survey.

Your broker's website should be able to provide the calendar of fundamental announcements, if not then please email us and we will be able to provide the best websites to look at for this information.

So how do you trade the FAs? Early in my FOREX career I was 100% technical, making good profits from this, until such time as the technically strong currency was crushed following release of FAs.

Today I consider fundamental, technical, and market sentiment simultaneously; each one provides important clues. For example, if I think the market sentiment is changing to USD positive and it's starting to look good on the charts, and a great number for the USD is being released, this to me is a perfect buy signal; it looks good and the news says it will be good; in a game of probability I can't imagine a better trade set up. This kind of holistic view is essential for FOREX trading success in my opinion. Consider this, 95% of new FX traders lose and 95% of new FX traders rely solely on technicals. That's enough of a reason for me not to rely exclusively on technical analysis only!

My experience has been that once a strong move is generally underway, following the release of FA's, a lot more can be made going with the move as it kicks into high gear, of course at this point I will also consider the charts, and the support and resistance levels.

GBPUSD – 4 hour chart

Source: eSignal. www.eSignal.com

On the above 4-hour chart release of FAs, being Dollar negative sees the Cable making an explosive move initially, but the rally stops precisely at a double top – Who would have guessed? Then followed by the pound getting crushed. On the failure of a breakout – I was quite happy to go short for over a hundred-pip ride south.

This is where doing your homework will help you tremendously. Before the release of FAs I will always sit down and look at the charts, in all time frames and look at the trend lines, with support and resistance levels, also look at the pivot points for the day.

GBP USD 5 minute Chart

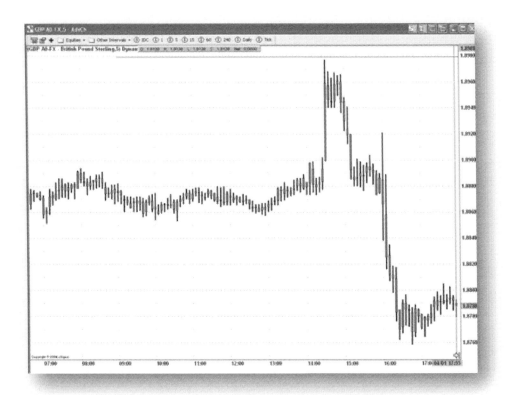

Source: eSignal. www.eSignal.com

As you can see from the above 5 minute chart, the Dollar got crushed, The Cable moved up nearly 100 pips on the 5 minute chart – then settled in a rectangle channel for a 30 pip range. Once this range is broken to the downside, there is a move south of nearly 200 points. A good short entry would have been at the break of the channel. Once again, another example of Technical analysis and breakout pattern on the FA days.

Due to so much volatility in forex, many Bindal FX members do a straddle trade on the day of a major FA, and this strategy works the majority of times. In fact with this system – you are in profit if you were wrong 50% of time. So in the above chart, before the release of the FA, the trader goes long on one account, and then also goes short on the other account. He targets 75 pips from each trade – and has a stop of 150 pips. On this basis you can only lose on one – not both – yet with volatility like the above chart – you can win on BOTH the trades. Surely a case of free money for 10 minutes work!

Paper trade, and see it for yourself. I have so far done 4 trades, won 2 (300 pips) and lost 2 (150 pips). Overall gain of 150 pips – not bad! Just for a few minutes' work. This strategy works so well when there is a big price move, but the price action failed to follow through and the price went back through the pre-release start point!

Example of a trade based on the above strategy would be - Refer to the chart of GBPUSD on the previous page;
Simultaneously do the following trade, before the release of FAs

On Account A
Go Long at   1.8885,
Target   1.8960 (75 pips)
Stop   1.8740 (150 Pips)

On Account B
Go short at   1.8880 (assuming a 5 pip spread)
Target   1.8810 (75pips)
Stop   1.9030 (150 pips)

May seem a silly trade to most, but tends to work time after time on most occasions. Most brokers do offer a hedging trade, whereby you can have a short and a long position on the same account.

As soon as the FAs are released, the Cable moves up nearly 100 pips, at this stage your long would have been filled for a 75-pip profit.

However, during the next 2 hours subsequently the Cable moves down by over 200 pips. At this stage your shorts on Acct. B has been filled with a profit of another 75 Pips.

Overall you have come out with a net gain of 150 pips, and you were risking 75 pips. That is a risk reward of 1: 2. With so much volatility, not a bad way to trade.

You should however appreciate that this strategy seems to work in the current very volatile markets. If however, the behaviour and the pattern of currencies change, than this strategy will not work. Try it out and paper trade it.

If it works, stay with it – and the day it stops working, look for something else.

CHAPTER 23
THE POWER OF FOREX OPTIONS

- **Option basics**

- **Call options**

- **Put Options**

- **Why trade options?**

- **Covered call**

- **Covered put**

- **Hedging your position using options**

- **How to repair a trading position**

"The power of Options strategies can offer a trader an opportunity to trade the markets without fear, and let the winners run for a maximum profit."

Jayendra Lakhani

THE POWER OF FOREX OPTIONS

Many traders think of stocks and index when they think of options; however the Forex market also allows the traders to benefit from these powerful strategies.

Options - Understanding the Basics

An option is a contract between two parties, the buyer and the seller of the option. The buyer of the option has the right but not the obligation, to buy or sell a security at a set price (strike price) and time (expiry date of the option), from the option seller.

The Option seller (writer) is obligated to sell the security should the buyer choose to exercise his right.

Still confused? The concept of an option is present in our day to day life. Say, for example, that you discover a house that you'd love to purchase. Unfortunately, you won't have the cash to buy it for another three months. You talk to the owner and negotiate a deal that gives you an option to buy the house in six months for a price of £500,000. The owner agrees, but for this right, you pay a premium of £5,000.

Now, consider two theoretical situations that might arise:

Scenario 1
It's discovered that the house is actually the true birthplace of a celebrity! As a result, the market value of the house skyrockets to £2 million. Because the owner sold you the option, he is obligated to sell you the house for £500,000. In the end, you stand to make a profit of £1,495K (£2 million - £500,000 - £5,000).

Scenario 2
While touring the house, you discover that the house is close to a proposed dump site for waste products. Though you originally thought you had found the house of your dreams, you now consider it worthless. On the upside, because you bought an option, you are under no obligation to go through with the sale. Of course, you still lose the £5,000 price of the option.

This example demonstrates two very important points. First, when you buy an option, you have a right but not an obligation to do exercise your option, IF it is in your favour. You can always let the expiration date go by, thereby the option becomes worthless. If this happens, you lose 100% of your investment, i.e. the premium paid to buy the option. Second, an option is merely a contract that deals with an underlying asset. For this reason, options are called derivatives, which means an option derives its value from something else. In our example, the house is the underlying asset. Most of the time, the underlying asset is a share, or an Index, a commodity or a currency.

Investors buy and sell options just like stocks. There are two basic types of options:

The call option
The put option

The Call Option

The call option is the right to buy the underlying security at a certain price on or before a certain date. Buying a call is similar to having a long position on a security. Buyers of the option expect the price of the security to go up before the expiry of the option.

Example;

On Thursday 28th September GBPUSD is trading at a spot price of 2.0230 and if you were very bullish on this currency pair, you could buy a call option. You are taking a very short term view of less than 2 days. You decide to buy the option expiring the next day. Your trade would look something like this:

Date: 28th Sep
Currency Pair   GBPUSD
Current Spot price $2.0230
Strike price: $2.0250
Option trade: Buy calls
Premium: 25 pips

Scenario 1

You were wrong and the price did not rise above your strike price. So in this case you would lose the 25 pips. This would be the maximum loss that you would sustain. The seller of the option would keep the entire 25 pips as his profit.

Scenario 2

You got it right and the price reached a maximum of 2.0490 the next day. This is 240 pips above the strike price. What are your options?

You can trade the options at any time before expiry; you can choose to take partial profits as the currency moves in your favour. You can close the position as soon as your target is achieved or you choose to close the bet as the signal may have reversed, or you could run the option till expiry, in which case you will be able to close the option at the price it expired.

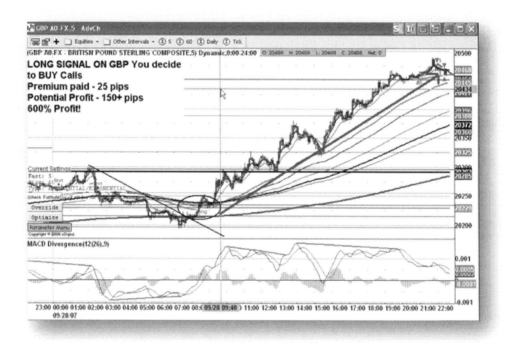

Many traders simply trade the option for a profit without actually buying the currency contract.

BUYING CALLS

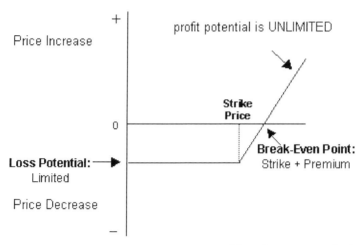

Volatility:
Increase = Positive Effect
Decrease = Negative Effect

Time Decay - results in options
value going down, as the expiry
date of the options aproaches.

245

The Put Option

The put option is the right to sell the underlying security at a certain price on or before a certain date. You would buy a put option if you were bearish of a currency pair and expected the price to head lower before the option reached expiration.

Example

On Tuesday 25th September CHF is trading at a spot price of 1.1720 and if you were very bearish on this currency pair, you could buy a daily PUT option. You are taking a very short term view of a day. Your trade would look something like this:

Date:	25th Sep
Currency Pair	CHF
Current Spot price	1.1720
Strike price:	1.1700
Option trade:	Buy PUTS
Premium:	15 pips

Scenario 1
You were wrong and the price did not fall below your strike price. So in this case you would lose the 15 pips. This would be the maximum loss that you would sustain. On the other hand the seller of the option would keep the entire 15 pips as his profit.

Scenario 2
You got it right and the price reached a maximum of 1.1635 during the day. This is 65 pips above the strike price. What are your options?

You can trade the options at any time before expiry; you can choose to take partial profits as the currency moves in your favour. You can close the position as soon as your target is achieved or you choose to close the bet as the signal may have reversed, or you could run the option till expiry, in which case you will be able to close the option at the price it expired.

25 Sept 2007 - London open
Short Signal
Spot @ 1.1720
BUY 1.1700 Daily Put
Premium 15 pips
Maximum profit @ 70 pips
450%

BUYING PUTS

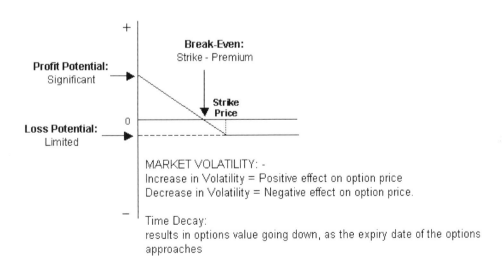

Profit Potential:
Significant

Loss Potential:
Limited

Break-Even:
Strike - Premium

Strike Price

MARKET VOLATILITY: -
Increase in Volatility = Positive effect on option price
Decrease in Volatility = Negative effect on option price.

Time Decay:
results in options value going down, as the expiry date of the options approaches

Participants in the Options Market?

There are 4 types of participants in the options market.

1. Buyers of calls – gives you a right to buy the security.
2. Sellers of calls – you have the obligation to sell the security.
3. Buyer of puts – gives you a right to sell a security.
4. Seller of puts – you have an obligation to buy a security.

Selling options is more risky if you do not know what are you are doing as it can involve unlimited risk. If the price goes up and you have sold a call option you have the obligation to deliver the security at the strike price. If you do not own the security then you have to buy it in the market at a loss.

Why trade options?

1. Your downside is limited to only the amount of option premium paid, so in the above example of the CHF your maximum loss was only 15 pips

2. You have unlimited profit potential. So in the example of the GBP call option, the price shot up by more than 200+ pips, whilst the signal was still long. Downside was very limited but you had unlimited profit potential.

3. Leverage - You may pay less margin upfront than compared to a spot forex position or buying the security outright.

4. You select the strike price and also the expiration date.

5. You can use your option positions to hedge against your open spot positions.

6. Trade during fundamental news – without risking lot of capital, you can trade during the release of fundamental news.

7. Flexibility – Options can be used in a wide variety of strategies and can be tailored to meet your risk profile, from a cautious strategy to even a high risk.

Disadvantages of Options

1. Buying options involves paying for time value. Sometimes you could still be right in the direction of the price movement, yet not profit from the move because of the time value paid. It is said that due to this time decay, the majority of options expire worthless, this applies to those traders who bought the options. Seller of options will benefit as they keep the premiums.

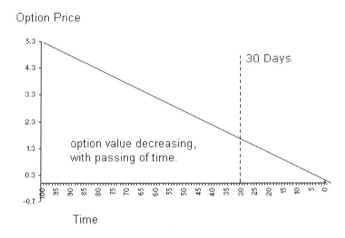

2. The premium varies according to the volatility. Often during high volatility, the options may be very expensive.

3. Options have an expiration date. Sometimes very difficult to predict the exact time period and the price movement to occur before the expiration of the options.

4. As soon as the option expires you have no position, so should the market then go in your favour you do not gain as the option has expired.

5. An option does not fluctuate in a 1:1 relationship like the spot market. This is because when you buy the option you start with paying for the time value. So effectively you are starting out with a loss, however as the option becomes more and more heavily in the money, the option value will fluctuate very closely with the pip value change. The term used to describe the relationship between the changes in the option price with the change in the price of the security is called Delta.

6. Unlimited Risk – Option writing can involve unlimited risk and should be avoided completely by amateur traders. Having said that this strategy is widely used by professional traders.

Intrinsic Value and Time Value

At this point it is worth explaining more about the pricing of options.

Intrinsic value – This is the value of an option when the option is exercised. It is defined as the difference between the options strike price and the actual current price.

Example;
Strike price   100.00
Current price   105.25
Intrinsic value   5.25

If the strike price is greater than the current price than the intrinsic value equals to zero;

Strike price   110.00
Current price   105.25
Intrinsic value   Zero

Your option would not be worth anything if it were to be exercised today. The intrinsic value will always be above zero.

Time Value – this is the second component of an option's price. It is defined as any value of an option other than its intrinsic value;

Example
Strike price   100.00
Current price   95.00
Options premium 1.00

Intrinsic value   Zero (because the current price is lower than strike price)
Time Value   1.00

Options that have zero intrinsic value are comprised entirely of time value. Time value reflects the probability that the option will gain in intrinsic value or become profitable to exercise before it expires.

Time value = Option premium – intrinsic value

Example;
Strike price   100.00
Current price   105.00
Option premium   7.50

Intrinsic value   5.00   (105.00 – 100)
Time value   2.50   (7.50 - 5.00)

Option Pricing - Pricing of options requires complex mathematical calculations and also several factors that impact on the premium. One is the relationship between the futures price and the strike price. The more an option is in the money, the more it is worth.

A second factor is volatility. Often during periods of uncertainty, the markets will be very volatile and this will be reflected in the price movements of the security. This volatility will stimulate the demand of options. The greater volatility means that the options writers demand higher premiums.

The third factor affecting the premium is the length of the option contract – expiration date. The longer the expiration date, the higher the time premium as the buyer of the option has more time in his favour for the price of the security to move in his direction.

COVERED CALL

Definition
The selling of a call option, while simultaneously holding an equivalent position in the underlying security.

Example;

You buy or own a security
Current price   100.00
Strike price   105.00
Options premium   1.50

This strategy is ideal for a trader who is taking a long term view of a bullish stance on the security, but would like to derive additional profits. By selling the out of the money option, giving him a buffer of £5.00, the trader is collecting a premium of £1.50.

In this example if the price is below the strike price before expiry than the option expires worthless and you keep the premium. You can keep repeating this exercise every day/week/month, and keep collecting option premiums. A successful outcome of a covered call strategy leads to lowering the holding cost of the security.

How can a covered call help?

With this strategy you assume the role of an options seller. However you are not going to take unlimited risk by selling a naked call option because you already own the underlying security. By doing a covered call you are protected against unlimited losses in the event the option goes deep in the money and is exercised.

When to use a covered call?

There are a number of reasons why traders use covered calls as part of their strategy;

1. Produce regular income from holding the security.
2. Regular income received reduces the holding cost of the security.
3. Profiting from the option premium due to the time decay, but the trader does not want to take unlimited risk by writing a naked call option.
4. Look for overvalued call options to benefit from time value.
5. Neutral to bullish view – The covered call strategy works best when you do not expect much volatility in price, either to the upside or the downside. Ideally you want to hold your security and consistently collect premiums thereby lowering your average holding cost each period.

How to improve the covered call

Covered call does not remove the risk to the downside. Although you are receiving a limited premium by selling the call, you are still exposed to a risk of a substantial market downturn. You can limit the downside by adopting the following steps;

Have a stop loss on your security, so this limits the amount of your loss. However once you are stopped out, you must ensure that you do close the call written as you do not want to be exposed to a sudden market reversal. The call written would be closed for a profit, as the market has gone in the opposite direction and also there would be time decay. The profit from the call would in some way compensate for being stopped out.

Buy a protective put – you are insuring against the market downturn, so in the event of a significant move in the market to the downside, your losses would be minimized as the puts would now generate a healthy profit. The protective put would have the effect of capping your downside until the expiration of your option.

What to do at expiration

1. If the option is out of the money, it will just expire worthless and will not be exercised. In this case no action required by you, you keep the premium as a profit.

2. Roll out – you could repeat the exercise again and write another option thereby collecting premiums.

3. If the option is in the money. The option is likely to be exercised and called away. But often many traders will tend to close the position before the expiry.

COVERED CALL TRADE EXAMPLES

On 15th June 2007 the Bindal FX system issues a long signal – swing trade. The technical indicators are looking very bullish and a long trader may want to hold the position indefinitely until the swing trade signal changes to short.

An aggressive trader can be on the long side, but can sell daily calls when the intraday system issues a short signal.

Often between the times of London Open and US open there is a significant time value in the daily options, this can be used to your advantage. The average at the money options would normally cost around 35 to 50 pips.

You can easily collect at least 350 pips during the 6 week period on the above GBP Bull Run, and just the premiums collected would amount to over a 1000 pips.

Finally on a bearish 1-2-3 the trader closes the long position for over 850 pip profit! Using the daily covered call strategy removes the fear of a loss and you are regularly collecting premiums from the market to lower your average entry cost of your long position.

Can Forex traders have their (profit) cake and eat it too? Although conventional wisdom states that you can't 'have your cake and eat it too!' the covered call strategy above has proven that you can!
In summation the covered call enables you to own a security, have room for profit, pocket daily premiums from selling calls and thereby be protected on the downside.

Using Covered Call for a volatile currency – GBPJPY

GBPJPY can offer excellent trading opportunities due to its volatility. But many traders stay away from this currency due to fear of a loss, and also not wanting to place wider stops. Often this currency can move 100 pips within few minutes.

Consider the following example;

Bindal FX system issues a long signal at 231.10, but placing a tight stop you run the risk of being stopped out. You may not want to risk 100+ pips on this long trade;

You may do the following;
Enter long @ 231.10 with a 100 pip stop
Simultaneously sell a weekly 28th Sep Call option and receive a premium of 95 pips, strike price 232.00.

Scenario 1

Price stays above the strike price of 232.00, you are guaranteed a profit of 185 pips (232.00 – 231.10 = 90 + 95 = 185 pips). The 185 pips is the maximum profit you can make, even though the currency goes up by nearly 400 pips.

Scenario 2

Let's assume that the price rises to only around 231.50.

Your profit will be 135 pips (231.50 - 231.10 = 40 + 95 = 135 pips) the call option you sold expires worthless and you keep the premiums. Yet again a low risk trade strategy.

Scenario 3

Let's assume that the price goes down to 230.50, so you have lost 60 pips from the long trade. But the call option will expire worthless and you keep the premium of 95 pips. So despite the market moving against you, you still make a profit of 35 pips! (95-60 = 35 pips profit)

Scenario 4

Let's assume that you get stopped out, so your loss is -100 pips. At this stage you would look to close your calls you sold. Your received 95 pips for it, but because the price has fallen and also due to the decay in time value you would be able to buy back the option for around 30 pips, thereby making a profit of 65 pips on the option.
Overall you lost 100-65 = loss of 35 pips, not bad on a swing trade GBPJPY.

Conclusion – This strategy would give you a maximum profit of around 185 pips and the lowest possible loss of approx 35. A risk reward ratio of over 1:5. Surely a great way to trade.

WARNING – On being stopped out, you must ensure that you close the call option for a profit.

COVERED PUT

Definition

The covered put, also known as selling a covered put, is a lesser known variant of the popular covered call option strategy. A covered put is the selling of a put option while being short an equivalent amount in the underlying security

Example;

You short a security and then sell a put option
Current price   100.00
Strike price   95.00
Options premium   1.50

This strategy is ideal for a trader who is taking a long term view of a bearish stance on the security, but would like to derive additional profits. By selling the out of the money option, giving him a buffer of £5.00, the trader is collecting a premium of £1.50.

In this example if the price is above the strike price before expiry than the option expires worthless and you keep the premium. You can keep repeating this exercise every day/week/month, and keep collecting option premiums. A successful outcome of a covered put strategy leads to averaging down the cost of the overall short position.

When to use a covered put?

There are a number of reasons why traders use covered puts as part of their strategy;

Produce income whilst shorting the security.
Regular income received reduces the holding cost of the security.
Profiting from the option premium due to the time decay.
Look for overvalued put options to benefit from time value.
Neutral to bearish view – The covered put strategy works best when you do not expect much volatility in price, either to the upside or the downside. Ideally you want to hold your short position security and consistently collect premiums thereby

improving your average short entry price.

If you are extremely bearish then you would not use this strategy as it would cap your profits.

What to do at expiration

1.) If the option is out of the money, it will just expire worthless and you keep the premium as a profit.

2.) Roll out – If you are still neutral to bearish, you could repeat the exercise again and write another option thereby collecting premiums.

3.) If the option is in the money. The investor will have the security put to them at the short put strike price. This can now be off set against the security you were short. But often many traders will tend to close the position before the expiry.

Cautions with this strategy:

1.) The maximum risk is infinite, as the security can keep going high.

2.) Most investors avoid shorting the stocks.

3.) If there are good fundamental news for the security, the price could rise dramatically thus it could result into a bigger loss than anticipated.

4.) You run the risk of missing out on the large gain should the security price crash.

COVERED PUT TRADE EXAMPLE

You short a security and then sell a put option
Current price   100.00   also the price of your short trade
Put Strike price   95.00
Put Options premium   1.50

Scenario 1

At Expiry the price is at 98. Your profit will be 3.50 (100 - 98 = 2.00 +1.50 = 3.50) the option expires worthless and you keep the premium. You are still short of the security and you can decide to carry on with the short position if you are bearish.

Scenario 2

At expiry the price is 90. The option will be exercised by the buyer so you must buy the security at 95.00 (strike price). You will profit because you already sold it at 100. Your overall profit will be 100-95 = 5 +1.50 = 6.50

In this case 6.50 is your maximum profit, you can simply not gain more than this amount. If however it was a normal short trade and not a covered put than your profit would be 10 (100-90).

Scenario 3

At expiry the price has risen to say 120. The put option will expire worthless and you keep the premium of 1.50. However as you were short and the price has risen to 120, your overall loss would be 18.50 (100-120 = -20 + 1.50 = -18.50 loss)

As you can see this can be a dangerous strategy if you do not manage it well. Obviously as soon as the signal reversed you would close the short position for a loss and also realize the profit from the put.

As with every strategy, it can be dangerous if you do not manage it. But if you know what you are doing than even a covered put can give you handsome profit.

I use this strategy a lot on GBPJPY; because of the volatility the put option prices are often very expensive. So when I have an iron clad signal, I will combine it with a covered put.

Have a look at the following trade example using covered put strategy;

Bindal FX system issues a Short signal at 232.80, but placing a tight stop you run the risk of being stopped out. You may not want to risk 100+ pips on this short trade;

Scenario 1

You may do the following;
1.) Enter short @ 232.80 with a 100 pip stop
2.) Simultaneously sell a weekly 28th Sep put option and receive a

premium of 210 pips, strike price 232.00.

Two days later the prices goes down by nearly 300 pips, and when the price is at 230.50, a buy signal is issued. The puts are deep in the money, but at the same time it would have lost some of the time value and the delta of the option would have gone up. The 232 put option may be worth 320 pips

You could at this stage, close the shorts at 230.50, thereby banking a profit of 230 pips on shorts. You could also close the puts at a loss of 110 (320-210). So overall you still make a profit of 120 pips from the covered put.

Scenario 2

Let's assume the price closes at 233.50 at expiry. Your overall profit & loss position would be as follows;

Loss on the short trade 232.80-233.50	-70
Put expires worth less; you keep the premium	+210
Overall	+140 profit.

Yet again this example illustrates the power of option strategies, the spot price went against you, yet you still ended up with a profitable trade.

HEDGING YOUR POSITIONS

Options can be used as an insurance policy to hedge your Long or Short positions.

Example; - Hedge for a Short.

This was a live trade taken by a Bindal FX member during one of the live trading Webinar sessions;

Date: 28th Sep
Currency pair   CHF
Strategy: Short
Short entry   1.1710
Hedge Call   1.1750   Strike price
Option premium   10 pips

If the price goes up above the strike price the maximum loss will be 50 pips
(1.1750-1.1710 = 40 +10 = 50)

The trader will not lose more than 50 pips no matter how high the price goes up.

The price subsequently fell to a low of the day of 1.1620. Before the market close the position was closed for a profit of 70 pips on the short trade.

HEDGING A LONG POSITION;

The following trade was taken live by Bindal FX members during a live trading webinar;

Date: 28th Sep
Currency pair   GBP
Strategy: Long
Long entry   2.0305
Incremental profit 30 pips   50% position closed for 30 pip
profit
Hedge Put   2.0300   Strike price
Option premium   13 pips

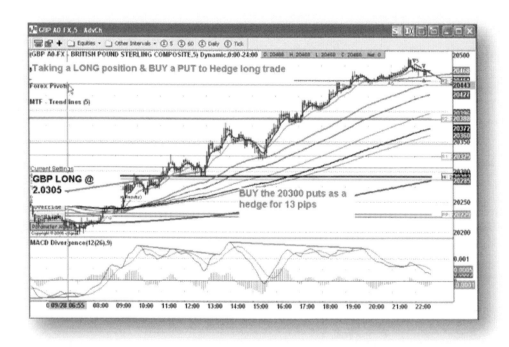

After taking an incremental profit of 30 pips and hedging the remainder of the position with buying a put, the trader was in a WIN WIN position. No matter what happened to the price, he can simply not lose on this trade!

The position finally closed for a profit of 150+ pips. The purchase of the puts gives the trader the confidence to run the profits to the maximum.

HOW TO REPAIR AN OPTIONS TRADE THAT WENT WRONG

The following trade was taken live by Bindal FX members during a live trading webinar;

Currency pair	EUR
Strategy:	Short Buy PUT options
Option Expiry:	28 Sep
Strike Price:	1.3850
Premium	52 pips
Incremental profit	35 pips 50% position closed for 35 pip profit

After banking an incremental profit of 35 pips, the net cost of the remainder of the option position was 52-35 = 17 pips. Therefore your total investment is now only 17 pips.

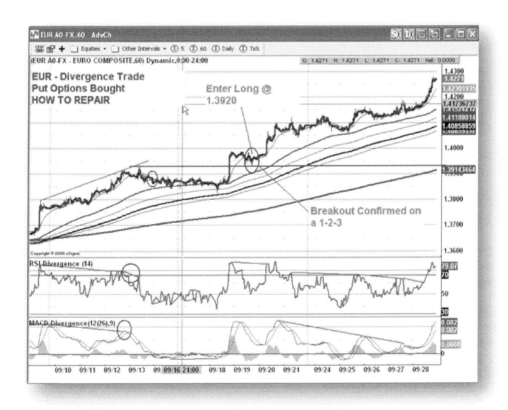

271

A put option taken on the basis of a Bearish Divergence signal. Subsequently there was a breakout. The breakout was confirmed with a bullish 1-2-3 setup. Long trade recommended at 1.3920.

The put option purchased, was now being used as a protection to the long trade.

At the expiry of the ut option on 28th Sep 2007, the signal was still long. But at this stage the spot long trade closed for a +300 pip profit. A powerful strategy illustrating how a put option trade was repaired on a breakout.

CHAPTER 24
CONFLUENCE OF
INDICATORS

Success in trading is down to having the discipline in following your rules and when you are able to do this the probability of success is greater. Your trading plan must be followed with ruthless discipline, and as always follow your golden rule: No Signal No Trade.

In this book, Forex Mastery – A Child's Play, I have discussed some very easy yet powerful trading strategies, and if you follow them exactly as described in this book, you will succeed. Trading need not be difficult, it is easy and there is a lot of money to be made from the markets – you just have to be patient and wait for an iron clad signal. In trading, it is very important that you not only preserve your capital, but you must be looking to increase your equity on a consistent basis.

Some of the strategies discussed in this book are;

1. Chart & Candle patterns.

2. Moving Average crossover system.

3. MACD Divergence system.

4. RSI trend line breakout system.

5. 1-2-3 retracement system.

6. Forex Pivot & Fibonacci Retracements.

7. The Power of 200 Ema.

An iron clad trade will come when you are patient and incorporate all or most of the above strategies together. Where you see a 'confluence of indicators' all pointing in the same direction, that is precisely the moment you want to take action. At other times, it is best not to trade, and save your trading account to see another day.

Let us look at the following Chart on the EURUSD, an Excellent Long signal issue for Position Trading on 22nd August 2007, at an entry price of 1.3480.

So what was the confluence of indicators? As always you have to take a top down approach.

1. Daily chart – A bullish 1-2-3 confirm and support at the 200 EMA. A break of the RSI trend line from extreme to extreme.

2. 4h chart – Break of a trend line resistance, break of RSI trend line, RSI divergence, a 1-2-3 pattern confirmed with the break of 2-3 resistance line.

3. 60 Min Chart – Very strong support at 1.3450. Multiple bottoms at this level.

4. 15 Min Chart – Bounce of a pivot point, followed by an EMA crossover, macd divergence, a bullish 1-2-3 setup, Fibonacci retracement of 61.8% exactly at the central pivot line, MACD above the waterline, support at the 200 ema. – 15 min chart is as follows:

EUR 15 Min Chart – 22nd Aug 2007

Having done the top down approach from the Daily right down to the 15 min chart, we would use the lower time frame to pull the trigger. All the time frames were bullish, and also lots of confluence of indicators.

Clearly when you have so many reasons to go long, all pointing in one direction then often you will have an explosive move. This has resulted in a bull run of over 600 pips.

The above analysis illustrates the merits of waiting for an iron clad trading signal, and when it comes you have to pounce. These are not unique signals nor are they rare, similar signals can be seen every week.

CHAPTER 25
POWER OF 200 EMA

The Power of 200 ema – this indicator is my all time favourite, and as I have often mentioned to my graduate members, you can devise a simple trading system using the power of 200 ema.

This strategy will work in all time frames, right from the 1 min charts to a Daily chart. Take a note of whether the price is above or below the 200 ema to give you a sense of price direction. The moving averages are a trend direction indicator and I consider the 200 EMA to be one of the most important.

The 200 EMA can be used in the following ways;

1. Breakout system

2. Dynamic support/resistance

How to use the 200 EMA?

Moving Average Breakout – When the price breaks the 200 EMA to the upside, the emphasis is to be on the long side and a move below the 200 EMA than we are looking to be on the short side.

The above chart on EURUSD using the 5 minute chart perfectly illustrates the breakout and how you can trade it to your advantage. After the breakout look for confluence of indicators, and the entry must be on a 1-2-3 setup or a retest of the 200 EMA.

200 EMA as dynamic support and resistance

Trading the bounces of the 200 EMA is one of favourite entry points. The 200 EMA often acts as a very strong dynamic support & resistance point, and the bounces can be used as a signal or trigger.

The 200 EMA can also be used as a target price as well. Always take a down to top approach, so for example if you see a break of 200 EMA on a 5 minute chart than switch your focus on what it does on a 15 minute chart and then on a 30 minute and so on. Often on a strong move you will see that gradually the 200 EMA on each of the time frames will break, finally you will end up with one chart time frame which may provide resistance/support.

Have a look at the following chart of the EURUSD, as at Sept 2007, it was on a great Bull Run and it was at all time highs.

The Chart also plots the 200 ema of the 1 min, 5, 15, 30, 60 and the 4hour charts – all on one 5 minute chart. As you can see the price is firmly above all the 200 EMAs of all the chart time frames. Also when the Bull Run is over, each of the 200 EMA will become targets. Finally you will see a Crossover of the 200 EMA lines all converging. This point could act as a dynamic support/resistance. A break would result in a big bear move.

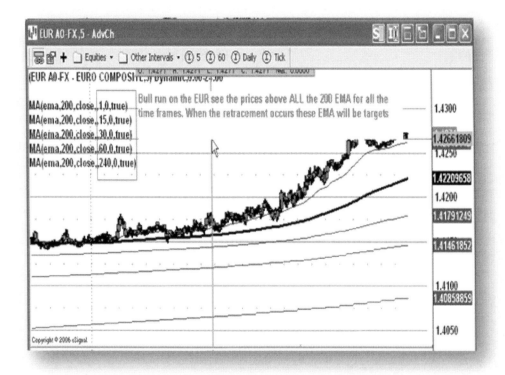

This simple system can offer a very powerful system to trade, you must do your own back testing, as you will feel much more confident if you are able to see the behaviour of the 200 EMA. If you keep it simple, you will not get paralysed with thousand of different signals.

When the prices are above all the EMAs, use the retracement bounces to take a position on the long side.

And Finally

Everything discussed in this book would be irrelevant if you choose not to take any action, if you choose to sabotage your life again and again. You have within you an immense potential to do the extraordinary things in life.

To achieve this potential you have got to have the DESIRE, your heart's desire, YOUR CORE DESIRE

PART 3
DEVELOP
MENTAL FITNESS

CHAPTER 26
YOUR DESIRES

"Desire is the starting point of all achievement, not a hope, not a wish, but a keen pulsating desire which transcends everything."

"When your desires are strong enough, you will appear to possess superhuman powers to achieve".

"First you fuel the desire, and then the desire will fuel you".
Above quotes from Napoleon Hill

Why do so many traders fail in this business and as a result never achieve true freedom and wealth?

- They quit.

- They did not follow the rules.

- They did not have the skills.

However, what is more important is the question, why do they not succeed when so many others do? The simple answer is that those who do succeed have a burning desire to do well. You will get a burning desire, when your desire to accomplish a task is at a core level of 100 on a scale of 100. When the intensity is so great, you must accomplish the task on hand, it dominates your thoughts each day.

If success in trading means paying off that credit card, or buying a house or firing your boss then you are lacking core desire. The truth is many traders do not treat trading as a business but as a hope. Hope is never backed by a true desire so the probability of a failure is high.

What is it at the very core of your being that you desire most? This is what I call a Core Desire.

Core desire creates intense and burning desire that originates from your heart, the power within you. The heart is set on achieving what you desire most. Your core desire is something that you love and are passionate about.

"Success is not the key to happiness. Happiness is the key to success. If you love what you are doing you will be successful."

Albert Schweitzer

Your heart-set is a much more accurate guide and source of success than your mind-set, so follow your heart. The heart-set desires have more imagination, as a result you will find a way to achieve your goals, our true feelings of emotions come from the heart. It is your core desires that get you excited.

So long as you focus on your desires you will succeed, you have to be wholehearted in achieving your goals. Half-hearted will only get you half way.

My question is: what is the desire level to achieve your trading success? Is it 50? (Like most people) Is it 75? (Not enough) Is it 90? (Not enough) or is it 100? – The only number that will produce results.

What would you be willing to give and sacrifice to succeed in trading? I hope the answer is "whatever it takes"; because I promise you that the end result is worth the sacrifice.

Knowing what one wants in life is not enough, if it was then the majority of plans and goals would not go unachieved. You must add the vibration of burning desire to your goals. It is the burning desire that empowers your thoughts and beliefs

My blunt advice is that you change your mindset today to get involved. Take full responsibility for your journey to achieve trading mastery.

Every human being has the same force of desire and determination that all successful people have. Follow these four simple steps and watch the desire come alive within you.

1. Write down a clear and concise statement on what it is that you wish to achieve. Using the SMART goal setting criteria.

2. Outline what actions you intend to take, what sacrifices you intend to make in order to achieve this objective.

3. Absolutely ensure that you have 100% dedication in following through with total commitment.

4. Read this statement aloud three times a day. As you read the statement visualise yourself achieving your goals.

"There is a power under your control that is greater than poverty, greater than the lack of education, greater than all your fears and superstitions combined. It is the power to take possession of your own mind and direct it to whatever ends you may desire."

Andrew Carnegie

SUMMARY & ACTION POINTS

1.) Why did you choose to trade Forex?

2.) Do you know what your heart desires? What would you like to achieve that you do not have now?

3.) If you achieved that, what would it give you that you don't have now?

4.) Keep asking yourself the same question after each answer, until you start getting the emotional responses. – Heart-set

5.) What would you be willing to give and sacrifice to succeed in trading?

CHAPTER 27

POWER OF THE SUBCONCIOUS MIND

"Whatever the mind can conceive and believe, it can achieve."

Napoleon Hill

We are all born to lead successful lives, we have within us to achieve extraordinary things in life. One of the ways we can condition our minds is by effective use of the subconscious mind. What your mind thinks, sees, believes, feels is all sent to your subconscious mind. Your subconscious mind then works with the universe to acquire your desires, for this to work you need to send the right messages to your subconscious mind – you have to take control of your mind.

The mind is a creature of habit so it becomes your responsibility to feed it with positive emotions and thoughts.

Affirmations
Affirmations are positive statements that describe a desired situation, and when repeated many times will trigger the subconscious mind into positive action. In order to ensure the effectiveness of the affirmation, they have to be repeated with great intensity and a burning desire that the desired situation has been achieved.

Examples of positive affirmations:

1. When I am trading I feel calm and relaxed.

2. My financial net worth increases each day as a result of my trading success.

3. The more money I have the more money I have to give.

4. I am like a magnet to money.

5. I am a powerful profitable Forex trader.

6. I focus on my golden rule of No Signal – No Trade.

7. I only trade on a confirmation of a 1-2-3 pattern.

Visualisations

Imagination is your ability to create a mental picture or a feeling of something that you want. Visualisation is using your imagination to create a positive outcome of your goal.

Let us take a few minutes to achieve your goals in your mind. Sit comfortably, relaxed with controlled deep breathing. Close your eyes and now focus on the mental pictures. Imagine the life that is exactly as you want it, what would you do each day? With whom would you be? The success of your career, see yourself enjoying the fun and leisure activities.

If you can see the goal in your mind you make it a reality. Visualisation is the first step to bringing a dream to your life.

For creative visualisation to work, you must have the desire in your heart that the goal is being realised. You must also have belief in your goal being achieved, there must not be any doubt whatsoever in your mind.

30 day formula to success

1. Spend 5 minutes, three times a day reading your affirmations.

2. Ensure that you are relaxed and free from any disturbance.

3. Whilst reading your affirmations, visualise the goals being achieved.

4. Focus on the positive emotions of how you feel and what you do.

5. Do this for 30 days.

"It's the repetition of affirmation that leads to belief. And once that belief becomes a deep conviction, things begin to happen."

Claude Bristol

SUMMARY & ACTION POINTS

1.) What are the negative habits that are pulling you down?

2.) What are the positive habits that you wish to have?

3.) Make a list of your positive affirmations that can lead to positive habits.

4.) Follow the 30 day formula to success – reading the affirmations with visualisations.

CHAPTER 28
THE POWER OF PRANAYAMA

"When the breath wanders the mind also is unsteady but when the breath is calmed the mind too will be still."

Svatmarama – Yoga Teacher

THE POWER OF PRANAYAMA

Prana – Life energy
Yama – Discipline

Pranayama is a Sanskrit word often translated as a control of life force (prana), in yoga it is translated as breath control. Pranayama techniques should be practiced under the guidance of a teacher or your medical practitioner. The way you breathe is the way you live. Full, free breathing is the key to enhancing physical, emotional and spiritual well-being.

Breathing fully and freely is our birthright. If you watch a baby breathe, you will see a remarkable sight. With each inhale, the baby's belly fills with air like a balloon, the pelvis rocks forward, the legs open. The chest rises and then falls. It is the way we were meant to breathe.

Sitting and breathing evenly can be a means of tapping deeper resources within us. Breathing is one of the most profound and direct ways we have of changing or tuning our chemical and biological state to affect our neurology.

Deep, relaxed breathing promotes calmness and helps to relax our mind. When breathing in, breathe deeply into your stomach, hold the breath for a few moments, and exhale very slowly. Repeat the process several times. You will notice an instant sense of increased calmness.

This kind of breathing also helps when you find yourself emotionally overwhelmed. Deep breathing will help you to let go of stress and restore mental and emotional equilibrium, enabling you to handle the situation more effectively.

Pranayama and Trading

The power of Pranayama can immensely help a trader to be focused and relaxed. One of the most challenging aspects of trading is self control. One of the easiest and effective changes in your trading is to learn to control your breathing and posture. We need to breathe in order to think and function properly.

When you are sitting in front of your trading screen, breathing and posture is the last thing in your mind. In this situation what most traders would do is to constrict their breathing and shut off all the good oxygen delivery.

There are a number of breathing techniques that you can use, which will enable you to relax and gain control so that you are able to focus on your trading. It is very important that for medical reasons you seek medical guidance or that you receive expert guidance from a qualified yoga teacher.

Recommended reading;

Swami Ramdev Yoga
http://www.swamiramdevyoga.com/

Art of Living
http://www.artofliving.org/

Brahmakumaris
http://www.bkwsu.org/index_html

"The most important pieces of equipment you need for doing yoga are your body and your mind"

Rodney Lee – Yoga

SUMMARY & ACTION POINTS

1.) Learn the basics of Pranayama and breathing techniques?

2.) Spend at least 15 minutes daily meditating and doing simple breathing exercises.

GOALS:
Dreams With a Deadline

Conceive
Believe
Achieve

"Our plans miscarry because they have no aim. When a man does not know what harbour he is making for, no wind is the right wind."

CHAPTER 30 – CREATE A WINNING TRADING PLAN

"The most important element of a Master Trader is having a Trading Plan. Amateur traders have trouble making entry or exit decisions; they are totally confused because they really don't know what they are doing. They do not have a plan and a set of rules to guide them. And when they make a decision they are often wrong!"

By Jayendra Lakhani
Author and Trader

Creating a Winning Trading Plan

A trading plan is perhaps the most overlooked trader's tool. As a matter of fact the majority of traders do not have a trading plan. No wonder 90% of traders lose money. Many people are just too lazy to sit down and draw a plan. In fact 50% of you reading this may NEVER sit down to write a plan.

Once you have written a plan, you must have belief that your plan will work, otherwise there will be no discipline to follow it. Discipline is the key to succeed in Trading, just because you have a trading plan does not mean that success is assured, but without a plan you are likely to fail.

I always say to my students, that when you write a plan, write it as if your trading plan will be scrutinised by your boss and that your job will depend on it. Be very detailed and realistic in your plan, often I have seen that people are seeking to gain 500% return on investment on a monthly basis! This is unrealistic, even allowing for a 100:1 leverage!

Also many traders have so many strategies and countless indicators to work on, this leads to indecision and confusion – Analysis Paralysis. You must limit your strategies to a manageable level.

So what is a strategy? These are absolute set of rules which you follow each and every time you see a setup or a chart pattern, so your golden rule should be No Signal – No Trade!

You must have sound money management rules, because this will ensure success. You have to define acceptable loss, identify your entry and exit levels, and carefully calculate your risk/reward ratio. Sound money management principles will help you to minimise your losses, maximise your gains and keep you in the game.

Trading the markets should be treated like a business; it does not matter whether you trade full time or part time. Just as a business has pans and goals so should you as a trader. You need to define your goals, identify your expenditure and lay out your trading strategies that you will use to reach these goals.

Your trading plan must be followed with absolute discipline in order to succeed. The trading plan should be tailored to suit your personality, ability and resources. It should be YOUR plan and unique to your style of trading.

I will go through a template that I use as part of training Forex traders.

Your answers should not be vague and a simple one liner. The more you expand with relevant information, the more it will help you in your trading.

There is no room for ambiguity in your plan. Also where possible, always define and qualify your statements.

This usually means posing questions – what, when, where, why or how.

For example if you were trading the EUR. Why the EUR and not Cable?

What are the components of a good trading plan?

Have you got the skills to be a trader?

- Mental preparation - how do you prepare mentally to trade?

- Set risk level – your attitude to risk.

- Set goals – what targets do you intend to achieve.

- What research and homework you do before entry and exit? – Do you have a reason to trade?

- Your entry and exit rules – have discipline to stick to your rules.

- You should review your day, week, month and year – write your conclusions in your trading diary.

- Record keeping – you should be able to compute your financial accounts, showing your net profits.

- Trading journal? Do you keep a record of all your trades? With reasons?

Quality questions will lead to a good trading plan

"A major stimulant to creative thinking is focused questions. There is something about a well-worded question that often penetrates to the heart of the matter and triggers new ideas and insights."

Brian Tracy

You passed a major hurdle, when you made a decision to create a trading plan. This is an important step in itself.

In order to create a winning trading plan, countless hours must be spend on planning itself. Planning is made easier if you are focussed, and motivated. This will come with quality questions; as a result you will get quality answers. If you ask you shall receive.

Your business as a Forex trader will succeed, only if ask the right questions about markets and strategies, and learn from it.

"He who asks a question is a fool for five minutes; one who does not ask a question remains a fool forever." – Chinese Proverb.

The human brain is the most powerful computer and no machines can ever replace it, yet sadly we do not use it to its full capacity. If you are not doing well as a trader than what question will you ask yourself? The answer of which will determine your future!

For example you could ask, what plan of action do I need in order to achieve my ultimate goal of financial freedom through trading? The question you will ask will determine where you focus, how you think, what are your feelings, and what will you do?

One trader I mentored recently asked a quality question, how could I succeed while 90% of traders are failing? How can I turn it around? He asked this question with great intensity and expectation. He went about writing a book for himself on a trading plan, using the detailed template in the Bindal FX home study manual (www.4x4u.net). The end result was a 100-page trading plan document. This trader has not looked back! It all started from a focussed quality questions. Quantity is not important, but what is important is the relevance of information in your plan.

Many traders want to achieve financial freedom, being their own boss, than why don't you get leverage: ask yourself, " If I don't become a master trader, what price will I have to pay, what will it cost me in the long run and what impact it will have on my life? " and " How will my life be transformed, if I get this right?

I do hope that this will get your brains ticking.........

You can download a free template on how to create a Winning Trading Plan from the following website:

http://www.4x4u.net/index.asp

Finally, remember that you can achieve Forex Mastery. By attending the Forex Mastery course you have demonstrated that you are a person of action and committed to change your life for the better. More importantly, you are committed to making a difference in your life or the lives of those you care about.

"Our deepest fear is not that we are inadequate. Our deepest fear is that we are powerful beyond measure.

It is our light, not our darkness, that most frightens us. We ask ourselves, who am I to be brilliant, gorgeous, talented, and fabulous? Actually, who are you not to be? You are a child of God.

Your playing small doesn't serve the world. There's nothing enlightened about shrinking so that other people won't feel insecure around you. We are all meant to shine, as children do. We are born to make manifest the glory of God that is within us. It's not just in some of us, it's in everyone.

And as we let our own light shine, we unconsciously give other people permission to do the same. As we are liberated from our own fear, our presence automatically liberates others."

Marianne Williamson

Printed in Great Britain
by Amazon